★ ★

MACMILLAN LITERA

American Stories

edited by Lesley Thompson
and Ceri Jones

Published by Macmillan ELT
Between Towns Road, Oxford OX4 3PP
A division of Macmillan Publishers Limited
Companies and representatives throughout the world

ISBN 978–0–2307–1689–6

All additional material written by Lesley Thompson and Ceri Jones

First published 2009
Text © Macmillan Publishers Limited 2009
Design and illustration © Macmillan Publishers Limited 2009
This version first published 2009

All rights reserved; no part of this publication may be
reproduced, stored in a retrieval system, transmitted in any
form, or by any means, electronic, mechanical, photocopying,
recording, or otherwise, without the prior written permission of
the publishers.

The author and publishers are grateful for permission to reprint the following copyright material:

Penguin Group (USA) Inc for the story "You were perfectly fine" from *Dorothy Parker: Complete Stories* by Dorothy Parker copyright © 1924-29, 1931-34, 1941, 1943, 1955, 1958, 1995 by The National Association for the Advancement of Colored People. Used by permission of Penguin, a division of Penguin Group (USA) Inc.;

David Higham Associates Limited for the story "The baby party" from *The Collected Short Stories of F Scott Fitzgerald* by F Scott Fitzgerald, reproduced with permission of David Higham Associates;

Dover Publications for the story "The Lost Phoebe" from *Short Stories* by ISBN by Theodore Dresier copyright © 1916 reproduced by permission of Dover Publications.

W W Norton & Company, Inc. and Bloomsbury for the story 'The Romantic' from *Mermaids on the Gold Course* by Patricia Highsmith, copyright © 1970, 1979, 1982, 1983, 1984 & 1985 by Patricia Highsmith. Used by permission of W W Norton & Company, Inc and Bloomsbury.

These materials may contain links for third party websites. We have no control over, and are not responsible for, the contents of such third party websites. Please use care when accessing them.

Cover by Corbis/ Bettmann (inset) & Getty/ Time & Life Pictures.

Printed and bound in Thailand

2011   2010   2009
6   5   4   3   2

Contents

Macmillan Literature Collections	4
Introduction	6
Using a dictionary	10

The Gift of the Magi — 12
by O Henry
A young couple exchange Christmas gifts

The Lost Phœbe — 32
by Theodore Dreiser
An old man cannot accept the loss of his wife

The Baby Party — 69
by F Scott Fitzgerald
A child's party has unexpected consequences

You Were Perfectly Fine — 98
by Dorothy Parker
A young man hears of his adventures on an evening out

The Romantic — 112
by Patricia Highsmith
A lonely woman finds a new way to create romance

Full Circle — 143
by Edith Wharton
A successful novelist decides to take on a secretary

Essay questions	188
Glossary	190
Language study index	198

Macmillan Literature Collections

Welcome to the *Macmillan Literature Collections* – a series of advanced-level readers containing original, unsimplified short stories written by famous classic and modern writers. We hope that these stories will help to ease students' transition from graded readers to reading authentic novels.

Each collection in the series includes:

Introduction

- an introduction to the short story
- tips for reading authentic texts in English
- an introduction to the genre
- a carefully-chosen selection of classic and modern short stories.

The stories

Each story is presented in three parts: the introduction and pre-reading support material; the story; and post-reading activities. Each part includes the following sections:

- *About the author* – in-depth information about the author and their work
- *About the story* – information about the story, including background information about setting and cultural references
- *Summary* – a brief summary of the story that does not give away the ending.

Pre-reading exercises

- *Key vocabulary* – a chance to look at some of the more difficult vocabulary related to the main themes and style of the story before reading the story
- *Main themes* – a brief discussion of the main themes, with questions to keep in mind as you read.

The story

You will find numbered footnotes in the stories. These explain cultural and historical references, and key words that you will need to understand the text. Many of these footnotes give definitions of words which are very formal, old-fashioned or rarely used in modern English. You will find more common, useful words and phrases from the stories in the *Glossary* at the end of the book. Words included in the *Glossary* will appear in **bold**.

Post-reading exercises
- *Understanding the story* – comprehension questions that will help you make sure you've understood the story
- *Language study* – a section that presents and practises key linguistic and structural features of authentic literary texts (you will find an index of the areas covered at the end of the book)
- *Literary analysis* – discussion questions that guide you to an in-depth appreciation of the story, its structure, its characters and its style.

In addition, at the end of each book there are:
- suggested *Essay questions*
- a comprehensive *Glossary* highlighting useful vocabulary from each story
- an **index** for the *Language study* section.

How to use these books

You can use these books in whatever way you want. You may want to start from the beginning and work your way through. You may want to pick and choose. The *Contents* page gives a very brief, one-line introduction to each story to help you decide where to start. You may want to learn about the author and the story before you read each one, or you may prefer to read the story first and then find out more about it afterwards. Remember that the stories and exercises can be challenging, so you may want to spend quite a long time studying each one. The most important thing is to enjoy the collection – to enjoy reading, to enjoy the stories and to enjoy the language that has been used to create them.

Answer keys

In many cases you can check your answers in the story by using the page references given. However, an Answer key for all the exercises will be available on the student's section of the Macmillan Readers website at www.macmillanenglish.com/readers

Introduction

What is a short story?

A short story is shorter than a novel, but longer than a poem. It is usually between 1,000 and 20,000 words long. It tells a story which can usually be read quite quickly. It often concentrates on one, central event; it has a limited number of characters, and takes place within a short space of time.

History of the short story

Stories and storytelling have existed for as long as people have had language. People love, and need, stories. They help us explain and understand the world. Before people could read or write, storytellers travelled from village to village, telling stories.

The first written stories developed from this storytelling tradition. Two of the best-known examples of early, written stories in Europe appeared in the 14th century. Chaucer's *Canterbury Tales* and Bocaccio's *Decameron* are both based on the same idea – a group of people who are travelling or living together for a short time, agree to tell each other stories. Their individual short stories are presented together as one long story.

The first modern short stories appeared at the beginning of the 19th century. Early examples of short-story collections include the *Fairy Tales* (1824–26) of the Brothers Grimm, in Germany, and Edgar Allan Poe's *Tales of the Grotesque and Arabesque* (1840), in the USA.

The American short story

The short story in the USA was strongly influenced by writers in Europe and Russia. Washington Irving (1783–1859) was the first important American writer of short stories. When he was Ambassador to Spain, he wrote one of his most famous collections of stories, *Tales of the Alhambra*. His stories show the influence of European folktale and legend.

Edgar Allan Poe (1809–49) was another famous writer of the period. He wrote stories of mystery and horror and some of the first detective stories.

In the late 19th century, printed magazines and journals became very popular and more and more short stories were published. The American short story became more realistic and was often based on direct experience. Popular authors included Theodore Dreiser, Nathaniel Hawthorne, Herman Melville, Mark Twain and Henry James.

By the 20th century, most well-known magazines included short stories in every issue, and the publishers paid a lot of money for them. In 1952 Ernest Hemingway's short story, *The Old Man and the Sea*, helped sell more than five million copies of the magazine *Life* in just two days. The writer Jack London had a contract with the magazine *Cosmopolitan* to write a story a month for a year at the rate of one thousand dollars per story. The money paid for short stories helped many writers to survive while they worked on their longer novels. Some writers, however, became known almost exclusively for their short stories. This is the case of O Henry, (1862–1910) who published ten collections of short stories in his lifetime.

Reading authentic literary texts in English

Reading authentic literary texts can be difficult. They may contain grammatical structures you have not studied, or expressions and sayings you are not familiar with. Unlike graded readers, they have not been written for language students. The words have been chosen to create a particular effect, not because they are easy or difficult. But you do not need to understand every word to understand and enjoy the story.

When you are reading in your own language you will often read so quickly that you skip over words, and read for the general effect, rather than the details. Try to do the same when you are reading in English. Remember that looking up every word you don't know slows you down and stops you enjoying the story.

When you're reading authentic short stories, remember:
- It should be a pleasure!
- You should read at your own pace.
- Let the story carry you along – don't worry about looking up every word you don't understand.
- Don't worry about looking up difficult words unless they stop you from understanding the story.
- Try not to use the *Glossary* or a dictionary when you're reading.

You might want to make a note of words to look up later, especially key words that you see several times (see *Using a dictionary* on page 10 for more tips on looking up and recording new words). But remember, you can always go back again when you have finished the story. That is the beauty of reading short stories – they are short! You can finish one quite quickly, especially if you do not worry about understanding every single word; then you can start again at the beginning and take your time to re-read difficult passages and look up key words.

Preparing yourself for a story

It is always a good idea to prepare yourself, mentally, before starting a story.
– Look at the title. What does it tell you about the story? What do you expect the story to be about?
– If there is a summary, read it. This will help you follow the story.
– Quickly read the first few paragraphs and answer these questions:
  Where is it set?
  When is it set?
  Who is the main character?
– As you read, concentrate on following the gist (the general idea) of the story. You can go back and look at the details later. You can use the questions at the end of the story (see *Understanding the story*) to help you understand what is happening.

Tips for dealing with difficult passages

Some stories include particularly difficult passages. They are usually descriptive and give background information, or set the scene. They are generally difficult to follow because they are full of detail. Try to read these passages quickly, understanding what you can, and then continue with the story. Make a note of the passage and come back to it later, when you have finished the whole story.

If, at any time, you are finding it difficult to follow the story, go back to this difficult passage. It may hold the answers to your questions.

Read through the passage again carefully and underline all the unknown words. Try to understand as much as you can from the immediate context and what you now know about the story. Then, look up any remaining words in the *Glossary* at the back of the book, or in your dictionary.

Tips for dealing with difficult words

- Decide if the word (or phrase) is important to the overall message. Read the whole paragraph. Do you understand the general meaning? Yes? Then the word isn't important. Don't worry about it. *Keep reading!*
- If you decide the word is important, see if you can work out its meaning from the context. Is it a verb, a noun or an adjective? Is it positive or negative? How would you translate it into in your own language? Underline the word or make a note of it and the page number, but *keep reading*. If it really is important, you'll see it again.
- If you keep seeing the same word in the story, and you still can't understand it, look in your monolingual dictionary!

Using a dictionary

Looking up words

Before you look up the word, look at it again in its context. Decide what part of speech it is. Try to guess its meaning from the context. Now look it up in your dictionary. There may be more than one definition given. Decide which one is the most appropriate. If the word is something very specific, eg the name of a flower or tree, you can use a bilingual dictionary to give you the exact translation.

Let's look at how this works in practice. Look at this short extract and follow the instructions below.

> ...there is a little valley or rather **lap** of land among high hills, which is one of the quietest places in the whole world. A small **brook** glides through it, with just murmur enough to **lull** one to repose*
>
> *literary: sleep or rest*
> The Legend of Sleepy Hollow by Washington Irvine

1 Look at the words in bold and decide what part of speech they are – noun, verb, adjective, etc.
2 Try to guess what they might mean.
3 Look at the extracts below from the *Macmillan English Dictionary for Advanced Learners*. Choose the most appropriate definition.

Words with more than one entry Sometimes the same word belongs to more than one word class: for example, *brook* can be both a noun and a verb. Each word class is shown as a separate entry. The small number at the end of the head-word tells you that a word has more than one entry.	**brook¹** noun a small river **brook²** verb not brook – to definitely not allow or accept something. **lap¹** noun 1 the top half of your legs above your knees when you sit down. 2 one complete turn around a course in a race PHRASE in the lap of luxury in very comfortable and expensive conditions
Idioms and fixed expressions Some words are often used in idioms and fixed expressions. These are shown at the end of the entry, following the small box that says PHRASE.	**lap²** verb 1 if an animal laps water, it drinks it gently with its tongue **lull¹** noun a quiet period during a very active or violent situation
Words with more than one meaning Many words have more than one meaning, and each different meaning is shown by a number.	**lull²** verb 1 to make someone feel relaxed and confident so that they are not prepared for something unpleasant to happen to lull someone into a false sense of security 2 to make someone relaxed enough to go to sleep

Dictionary extracts adapted from the Macmillan English Dictionary © Macmillan Publishers Limited 2002

Keeping a record

When you have looked in your dictionary, decide if the word is interesting or useful to you. If it is, make a note of it, and write down its definition. Make a note of the sentence where you found it in the story, then write one or two more examples of your own. Only do this for those words you think you will need to use in the future.

Here is an example of how you might record the word *lull*.

> 'with just murmur enough to lull one to repose'
> Lull – to make you feel relaxed enough to go to sleep
> e.g. The quiet sound of the waves lulled me to sleep
> The mother sang to her baby to lull it to sleep

Literary analysis

The *Literary analysis* section is written to encourage you to consider the stories in more depth. This will help you to appreciate them better and develop your analytical skills. This section is particularly useful for those students who are studying, or intending to study, literature in the medium of English. Each section includes literary terms with which you may or may not be familiar.

Macmillan Readers student's site

For more help with understanding these literary terms, and to find Answer keys to all the exercises and activities, visit the student's section of the Macmillan Readers website at www.macmillanenglish.com/readers. There you will also find a wealth of resources to help your language learning in English; from listening exercises to articles on acedemic and creative writing.

The Gift of the Magi
by O Henry

About the author

William Sydney Porter was the real name of the American short-story writer O Henry. Henry was very famous and popular in his day, and he is often referred to as the father of the modern short story. His stories have been translated into dozens of languages and are included in numerous anthologies. Even today, he remains one of the best-known and best-loved American short-story writers.

O Henry was born on September 11th, 1862 in Greensboro, North Carolina. His mother died of tuberculosis when he was three, so he was raised by his grandmother and his aunt. As a child, he loved reading. One of his favourite books was the classic short-story collection, *One Thousand and One Nights*.

At the age of 15 he left school and started working with his uncle in his drugstore[1], where he trained to be a pharmacist and a book-keeper[2]. At the age of 20 he left Greensboro for Texas and, after helping out on a sheep ranch, he moved to the town of Austin. There he had a variety of jobs. He worked as a pharmacist, a journalist and a bank clerk at the Austin National Bank. While he was living in Austin, he met and married Athol Estes. Two years later, they had a daughter, Margaret.

During his time at the bank in Austin, O Henry started publishing a humorous magazine called *The Rolling Stone*, which included short stories and humorous writings by Henry himself. When Henry lost his job at the bank, he began working on *The Rolling Stone* full time. But although the magazine was popular and sold well, it didn't make enough money to support his family. Henry eventually closed down the magazine and moved to Houston where he started writing for the *Houston Post*.

A few years after he moved to Houston, Henry was arrested and accused of embezzlement[3] at the Austin National Bank. The day before his trial he escaped, first to New Orleans and then to Honduras. He intended to wait there for his wife and daughter to join him and

1 *US*: chemist or pharmacy
2 person who records a company's financial accounts
3 the crime of stealing money that people trust you to look after as part of your work

start a new life. However Athol was too ill with tuberculosis to travel. When Henry heard that his wife was dying, he went back to Texas to be with her, and he eventually went on trial for embezzlement. He was found guilty.

He spent three years of his five-year sentence in a prison in Ohio, where he first started writing stories under the name of O Henry. He left prison in 1901; shortly after this, he moved to New York City, where he lived for the next eight years until his death in 1910. During that period he wrote over 300 short stories.

Henry's first collection, *Cabbages And Kings* appeared in 1904. The second, *The Four Million*, was published two years later, and included *The Gift of the Magi*. O Henry wrote more than 600 short stories. He published ten collections of short stories during his lifetime, and three more were published after his death.

His stories mainly deal with ordinary people and their lives. Many are based in New York City, but he also wrote about other places, including Texas and Honduras. Many of his stories have a surprise or twist[4] at the end. His stories tend to be humorous and optimistic, and some, like *The Gift of the Magi*, offer a moral lesson.

About the story

The Gift of the Magi is one of O Henry's best-known works. It was first published in a New York City newspaper in 1905. In 1906, it was published as part of *The Four Million*, a collection of stories which describe the lives of the ordinary people of New York City.

Background information

The story makes reference to two well-known biblical stories about gifts and their significance.

The Magi

The Magi, or the Three Wise Men, were, according to Christian tradition, three astrologer priests who travelled from the East to bring gifts to the baby Jesus in Bethlehem. They are also known as the Three Kings. They brought three gifts: gold, incense and myrrh. Each gift had a special meaning. Gold was for a king, incense for a priest and myrrh to prepare bodies for burial.

4 an unexpected conclusion to a story, often containing irony

King Solomon and the Queen of Sheba

King Solomon is a figure in the bible. He was famous for being a wise and good man as well as a very wealthy and powerful ruler. The Queen of Sheba, according to some religions (including Christianity, Islam and Judaism) was an extremely rich and powerful queen. According to various stories, she visited King Solomon with wonderful gifts and tested him with questions in order to judge how wise he was.

Summary

It may help you to know something about what happens in the story before you read it. Don't worry, this summary does *not* tell you how the story ends!

Della and Jim are a young, married couple. They live in a small, cheap flat in New York City in the early 1900s. They are very much in love.

It is Christmas Eve. Della wants to buy a Christmas present for Jim, but she has only got $1.87. She does not think this is enough to buy him the kind of present he deserves. So she decides to sell the thing she is most proud of – her beautiful, long brown hair – in order to raise the money she needs.

Della is paid $20 for the hair. This is enough for her to buy a special chain for Jim's most prized possession – a watch that was given to him by his father.

Della goes home to wait for Jim to come back from work. She washes her hair and worries that Jim won't like it now that it's so short. She sits at the kitchen table with Jim's Christmas present in her hand and waits for him to come home.

But when Jim arrives she finds that he too has decided to make a sacrifice in order to buy her a special present.

Pre-reading exercises
Key vocabulary

This section will help you familiarise yourself with some of the more specific vocabulary used in the story. You may want to use it to help you before you start reading, or as a revision exercise after you have finished the story.

Describing the flat

Almost all the action in the story takes place in Della and Jim's flat. Although the flat is not described in great detail, the few details given help us form a clear picture of the young couple's simple home.

1 Look at these sentences. Match the words in bold, which describe the features of the flat and its exterior building, with the definitions a–k below.

Della sits down to cry on a (1) **shabby** little (2) **couch**.

She looks at herself and her beautiful, long hair in a (3) **pier-glass**.

There was an (4) **airshaft** separating Della's flat from the flat opposite.

The (5) **janitor** had his room in the (6) **basement** at the bottom of the building.

Della could hear Jim's footsteps on the first (7) **flight** of stairs.

The (8) **letterboxes** were on the ground floor in the (9) **vestibule**.

The (10) **carpet** on the floor was old and (11) **worn**.

a) a vertical pipe or tube used for ventilating a kitchen or bathroom
b) the part of a building that is partly or completely below the level of the ground
c) a thick soft cover for the floor
d) a long, low, comfortable seat that two or three people can sit on
e) a set of stairs going from one level to another
f) mainly US: someone whose job it is to take care of a building (the usual British word is *caretaker*)
g) a small box in the hall of a block of flats where the mail (letters etc) is delivered (in a private house the letterbox is a hole in the front door through which the letters are posted)
h) a long, narrow mirror between two windows
i) an adjective used to describe something that is old and in bad condition

j) a room between the main door and the rest of a building or house, also known as the hall
k) an adjective used to describe something that looks old and damaged because it has been used a lot

How many of these features do you have in your house or flat?

Talking about money and the lack of it

Poverty and the importance of money is one of the main themes of the story. Look at the words below and their definitions; which are used to talk about:

1 not having any money?
2 spending very little money?
3 having (a lot of) money?

a) **beggar** (n) someone who is very poor and lives by asking people for food or money
b) **close dealing** (phrase) paying particular attention to how much money you spend
c) **income** (n) money that someone gets from working or investing
d) **mendicancy** (n) formal: the act of living by asking other people for food and money
e) **parsimony** (n) not wanting to give or spend money
f) **prosperity** (n) the situation of being successful and having a lot of money

Main themes

Before you read the story, you may want to think about some of its main themes. The questions will help you think about the story as you are reading it for the first time. There is more discussion of the main themes in the *Literary analysis* section after the story.

Material possessions

Money and material possessions play a central role in the story. The couple have two treasured possessions that have a sentimental value and beauty which is much greater than their material worth. However, by the end of the story, the two main characters understand that there is something that is much more important.

2 As you read the story, ask yourself:

a) What role does money play in the story?
b) Why are the two possessions so important?
c) What are they exchanged for?
d) What is the most important gift in the story?

Sacrifice and selfless love

Both of the main characters sacrifice something that is dear to them in order to give the person they love a gift.

3 As you read the story, ask yourself:

a) Whose sacrifice is the greatest? Why?
b) Were the gifts worth the sacrifices made to get them?
c) Were the sacrifices really necessary? Why/why not?
d) How else could they have shown their love? Would it have been as effective?

★ ★ ★ ★
The Gift of the Magi
by O Henry

One dollar and eighty-seven cents. That was all. And sixty cents of it was in pennies[5]. Pennies saved one and two at a time by bulldozing[6] the grocer and the vegetable man and the butcher until one's cheeks burned with the silent imputation[7] of parsimony[8] that such close dealing implied. Three times Della counted it. One dollar and eighty-seven cents. And the next day would be Christmas.

There was clearly nothing to do but flop down[9] on the shabby little couch and howl[10]. So Della did it. Which instigates[11] the moral reflection that life is made up of sobs[12], sniffles[13], and smiles, with sniffles predominating.

While the mistress of the home is gradually **subsiding** from the first stage to the second, take a look at the home. A furnished flat at $8 per week. It did not exactly beggar description[14], but it certainly had that word on the lookout for the mendicancy squad[15].

In the vestibule below was a letterbox into which no letter would go, and an electric button from which no mortal[16] finger could **coax** a ring. Also appertaining thereunto[17] was a card

5 a common, but unofficial, name for the one cent coin
6 to force someone to do something they don't really want to do, by being very determined
7 accusation
8 not being willing to give or spend money
9 to sit or lie down in a heavy way by relaxing your muscles and letting your body fall
10 to cry very loudly
11 *formal:* to make something start
12 the sounds made when crying noisily with short breaths
13 breathing in noisily through your nose because you are (or have been) crying
14 *phrase 'beggar description':* used to express shock at something that is extremely difficult to believe or describe
15 a play on words with the two meanings of *beggar*: 13 (above) and a poor person who lives by asking other people for money and food
16 *old-fashioned:* living
17 *old-fashioned:* belonging to

bearing the name "Mr. James Dillingham Young."

The "Dillingham" had been flung to the breeze[18] during a former period of prosperity when its possessor was being paid $30 per week. Now, when the income was **shrunk** to $20, though, they were thinking seriously of **contracting** to a modest and **unassuming** D. But whenever Mr. James Dillingham Young came home and reached his flat above he was called "Jim" and greatly hugged by Mrs. James Dillingham Young, already introduced to you as Della. Which is all very good.

Della finished her cry and attended to her cheeks with the powder rag[19]. She stood by the window and looked out **dully** at a gray cat walking a gray fence in a gray backyard. Tomorrow would be Christmas Day, and she had only $1.87 with which to buy Jim a present. She had been saving every penny she could for months, with this result. Twenty dollars a week doesn't go far. Expenses had been greater than she had calculated. They always are. Only $1.87 to buy a present for Jim. Her Jim. Many a happy hour she had spent planning for something nice for him. Something fine and rare and sterling[20] – something just a little bit near to being worthy of the honor of being owned by Jim.

There was a pier-glass between the windows of the room. Perhaps you have seen a pier-glass in an $8 flat. A very thin and very agile person may, by observing his reflection in a rapid sequence of **longitudinal** strips, obtain a fairly accurate conception[21] of his looks. Della, being slender, had mastered the art.

Suddenly she whirled from the window and stood before the glass. Her eyes were shining brilliantly, but her face had lost its color within twenty seconds. Rapidly she pulled down her hair and let it fall to its full length.

Now, there were two possessions of the James Dillingham Youngs in which they both took a mighty pride. One was Jim's gold watch that had been his father's and his grandfather's. The

---

18 *phrase 'fling to the breeze'*: to do something in a carefree way without worrying about the consequences
19 a piece of cloth used to apply make-up
20 *formal*: good, strong and reliable
21 *formal*: idea

The Gift of the Magi

other was Della's hair. Had the queen of Sheba[22] lived in the flat across the airshaft, Della would have let her hair hang out the window some day to dry just to depreciate[23] Her Majesty's jewels and gifts. Had King Solomon[24] been the janitor, with all his treasures piled up in the basement, Jim would have pulled out his watch every time he passed, just to see him pluck[25] at his beard from envy.

So now Della's beautiful hair fell about her rippling and shining like a **cascade** of brown waters. It reached below her knee and made itself almost a **garment** for her. And then she did it up again nervously and quickly. Once she **faltered** for a minute and stood still while a tear or two splashed on the worn red carpet.

On went her old brown jacket; on went her old brown hat. With a whirl of skirts and with the brilliant sparkle still in her eyes, she fluttered out the door and down the stairs to the street.

Where she stopped the sign read: "Mme. Sofronie. Hair Goods of All Kinds." One flight up Della ran, and collected herself, **panting**. Madame, large, too white, chilly, hardly looked the "Sofronie".

"Will you buy my hair?" asked Della.

"I buy hair," said Madame. "Take yer[26] hat off and let's have a sight at the looks of it."

Down rippled the brown cascade.

"Twenty dollars," said Madame, lifting the mass with a practised hand.

"Give it to me quick," said Della.

Oh, and the next two hours tripped by on rosy wings. Forget the hashed[27] metaphor. She was ransacking[28] the stores for Jim's present.

22 *biblical*: see background information p14
23 *formal*: to make something seem less important than it really is
24 *biblical*: see background information p14
25 phrase 'pluck at': pull on
26 *informal, spoken*: your
27 not very well constructed
28 to search thoroughly

She found it at last. It surely had been made for Jim and no one else. There was no other like it in any of the stores[29], and she had **turned all of them inside out**. It was a platinum fob chain[30] simple and **chaste** in design, properly **proclaiming** its value by substance alone and not by meretricious[31] ornamentation – as all good things should do. It was even worthy of The Watch. As soon as she saw it she knew that it must be Jim's. It was like him. Quietness and value – the description applied to both. Twenty-one dollars they took from her for it, and she hurried home with the 87 cents. With that chain on his watch Jim might be properly anxious about the time in any company. Grand as the watch was, he sometimes looked at it **on the sly** on account of the old leather strap that he used in place of a chain.

When Della reached home her intoxication[32] gave way a little to prudence and reason. She got out her curling irons[33] and lighted the gas and went to work repairing the **ravages** made by generosity added to love. Which is always a tremendous task, dear friends – a mammoth task.

Within forty minutes her head was covered with tiny, close-lying curls that made her look wonderfully like a **truant** schoolboy. She looked at her reflection in the mirror long, carefully, and critically.

"If Jim doesn't kill me," she said to herself, "before he takes a second look at me, he'll say I look like a Coney Island[34] chorus girl[35]. But what could I do – oh! what could I do with a dollar and eighty-seven cents?"

At 7 o'clock the coffee was made and the frying-pan was on the back of the stove hot and ready to cook the chops[36].

Jim was never late. Della doubled the fob chain in her hand and sat on the corner of the table near the door that he always

28 *US*: British word is *shops*
29 a short chain used to hold a pocket watch
30 seeming to be good, useful or important but not really having any value at all
31 *literary*: excitement
32 *old-fashioned*: metal rods that you heat and wrap your hair round in order to curl it
33 a beach resort in New York City
34 phrase *'chorus girl'*: a woman who dances in a chorus line
35 a small piece of meat with a bone in it, usually from a pig or sheep

entered. Then she heard his step on the stair away down on the first flight, and she turned white for just a moment. She had a habit for saying little silent prayers about the simplest everyday things, and now she whispered: "Please God, make him think I am still pretty."

The door opened and Jim stepped in and closed it. He looked thin and very serious. Poor fellow, he was only twenty-two – and to be burdened with a family! He needed a new overcoat and he was without gloves.

Jim stopped inside the door, as immovable as a setter[37] at the scent of quail[38]. His eyes were fixed upon Della, and there was an expression in them that she could not read, and it terrified her. It was not anger, nor surprise, nor disapproval, nor horror, nor any of the sentiments that she had been prepared for. He simply stared at her **fixedly** with that peculiar expression on his face.

Della **wriggled** off the table and went for him.

"Jim, darling," she cried, "don't look at me that way. I had my hair cut off and sold because I couldn't have lived through Christmas without giving you a present. It'll grow out again – you won't mind, will you? I just had to do it. My hair grows awfully fast. Say 'Merry Christmas!' Jim, and let's be happy. You don't know what a nice – what a beautiful, nice gift I've got for you."

"You've cut off your hair?" asked Jim, **laboriously**, as if he had not arrived at that **patent** fact yet even after the hardest mental labor.

"Cut it off and sold it," said Della. "Don't you like me just as well, anyhow? I'm me without my hair, ain't I[39]?"

Jim looked about the room curiously.

"You say your hair is gone?" he said, with an air almost of idiocy.

"You needn't look for it," said Della. "It's sold, I tell you – sold and gone, too. It's Christmas Eve, boy. Be good to me, for it went for you. Maybe the hairs of my head were numbered," she went

37 a kind of hunting dog
38 a small bird that people shoot and eat
39 *spoken, informal:* aren't I?

on with sudden serious sweetness, "but nobody could ever count my love for you. Shall I put the chops on, Jim?"

Out of his trance Jim seemed quickly to wake. He **enfolded** his Della. For ten seconds let us regard with discreet scrutiny some inconsequential object in the other direction. Eight dollars a week or a million a year – what is the difference? A mathematician or a wit[40] would give you the wrong answer. The magi[41] brought valuable gifts, but that was not among them. This dark assertion will be illuminated later on.

Jim drew a package from his overcoat pocket and threw it upon the table.

"Don't make any mistake, Dell," he said, "about me. I don't think there's anything in the way of a haircut or a shave or a shampoo that could make me like my girl any less. But if you'll unwrap that package you may see why you had me going a while at first."

White fingers and **nimble** tore at the string and paper. And then an ecstatic scream of joy; and then, alas[42]! a quick feminine change to hysterical tears and wails[43], necessitating the immediate employment of all the comforting powers of the lord of the flat.

For there lay The Combs – the set of combs, side and back, that Della had worshipped long in a Broadway window. Beautiful combs, pure **tortoise shell**, with jewelled rims – just the shade to wear in the beautiful vanished hair. They were expensive combs, she knew, and her heart had simply **craved** and **yearned** over them without the least hope of possession. And now, they were hers, but the tresses[44] that should have **adorned** the coveted adornments were gone.

But she hugged them to her bosom, and at length she was able to look up with **dim** eyes and a smile and say: "My hair grows so fast, Jim!"

40 someone who uses words in a clever and funny way
41 *biblical*: see background information p13
42 *old-fashioned*: used to say that you are sad about something and wished that it hadn't happened
43 a long high-sounding cry of sadness
44 *literary*: long hair that hangs down a woman's back

And then Della leaped up like a little **singed** cat and cried, "Oh, oh!"

Jim had not yet seen his beautiful present. She held it out to him eagerly upon her open palm. The dull precious metal seemed to flash with a reflection of her bright and ardent[45] spirit.

"Isn't it a dandy[46], Jim? I hunted all over town to find it. You'll have to look at the time a hundred times a day now. Give me your watch. I want to see how it looks on it."

Instead of obeying, Jim tumbled down on the couch and put his hands under the back of his head and smiled.

"Dell," said he, "let's put our Christmas presents away and keep 'em a while. They're too nice to use just at present. I sold the watch to get the money to buy your combs. And now suppose you put the chops on."

The magi, as you know, were wise men – wonderfully wise men – who brought gifts to the Babe in the **manger**. They invented the art of giving Christmas presents. Being wise, their gifts were no doubt wise ones, possibly bearing the privilege of exchange in case of duplication. And here I have lamely related to you the uneventful chronicle of two foolish children in a flat who most unwisely sacrificed for each other the greatest treasures of their house. But in a last word to the wise of these days let it be said that of all who give gifts these two were the wisest. O all who give and receive gifts, such as they are wisest. Everywhere they are wisest. They are the magi.

---

45 *literary*: showing very strong feelings of love
46 *mainly US, informal, old-fashioned*: excellent

Post-reading exercises

Understanding the story

1 **Use these questions to check that you have understood the story.**

Della at home

1 How had Della saved the $1.87?
2 Why did she count the money three times?
3 What had she saved the $1.87 for?
4 Why did Della start crying?
5 Who is Mr James Dillingham Young?
6 How do we know the two of them are in love?
7 Why did Della look at herself in the mirror?
8 What are the couple's two most prized possessions?
9 What decision had Della made as she looked in the mirror?
10 Was she happy about it?

Della's shopping trip

11 How much money did she get for her hair?
12 What was her hair going to be used for?
13 Where did she go next?
14 What did she buy?
15 Why did she choose that particular chain?
16 Why did Jim need it?
17 Why did she curl her hair?
18 Was she pleased with the results?
19 Was she worried that Jim might be angry with her?

Jim and Della

20 What was Jim's reaction when he saw Della's hair?
21 Why do you think he reacted like this?
22 What was Jim's Christmas present to Della?
23 What was her first reaction?
24 Why did she react like this?
25 What was her second reaction? Why?
26 Why did Della suddenly jump up?
27 What was Jim's reaction to his present?
28 What conclusion does the author draw from the story?

Language study

Grammar

Past perfect

The sequence of events is important in this story, as in any other. The past perfect is used to show that certain events happened before the main events of the story.

1 **Look at these examples.**

   *She **had been saving** every penny she could for months.* [page 19]
   *One was Jim's gold watch that **had been** his father's and his grandfather's.* [page 19]
   *Her heart **had** simply **craved** and **yearned** over them.* [page 23]
   *Jim **had not** yet **seen** his beautiful present.* [page 24]

2 **What is the significance of the verbs in bold for the story? Why is it important to emphasise that these things happened before the events in the story?**

Past perfect simple

The past perfect simple is formed using *had (not)* + past participle.

3 **Find three examples in the sentences above.**

The past perfect simple describes:
a) a state or situation that existed before a certain point in time in the past.
b) an action that happened before a certain point in time in the past.

Past perfect continuous

The past perfect continuous is formed using *had(not)* + *been* + verb + *-ing*.

4 **Find one example in the sentences above.**

The past perfect continuous describes an action that was in progress over a period of time before, or leading up to, a certain point in time in the past.

It is not used to describe states.

   It ~~had been being~~ his father's and his grandfather's.

5 Write the verbs in brackets in the past perfect simple or past perfect continuous.
1 Della (plan) for Christmas for a long time.
2 Jim (have) the same idea as Della.
3 She (sell) her hair to buy him a watch chain.
4 He (buy) her the hair combs she loved so much with the money he got when he sold his watch.
5 They (both/want) to give the other a wonderful surprise.
6 They (both/look forward) to this moment with excitement.
7 They (both/be) disappointed – not by their gifts, but by the fact that the gifts they (so carefully/choose) were no longer of any use.

6 Read through the story again, and find other examples of the past perfect.

Past perfect inversion in conditional sentences

Conditional sentences that describe the past are usually formed using *if* + past perfect / *would have* + past participle.

If Jim hadn't sold his watch, he wouldn't have been able to buy the combs.

We can drop the *if* by inverting the verb in the past perfect.

Had Jim not sold *this watch, he wouldn't have been able to buy the combs.*

Notice the position of (a) *had*, (b) *not*

7 Look at these two extracts from the story. Rewrite the beginning of the sentence without *if*.

If the queen of Sheba had lived in the flat across the airshaft, Della would have let her hair hang out the window some day to dry just to depreciate Her Majesty's jewels and gifts.

If King Solomon had been the janitor, with all his treasures piled up in the basement, Jim would have pulled out his watch every time he passed, just to see him pluck at his beard from envy.

8 Change the beginning of these sentences using inversion or *if* phrases.
1 If Della hadn't cut her hair, she could have used the combs.
2 Had she saved more money, she wouldn't have cut her hair.
3 Had Jim's salary not been cut from $30 to $20, he wouldn't have sold his watch.
4 If they had not bought each other any presents at all that Christmas, would they have been happier?

5 If Jim hadn't sold his watch, he would have been happy to use the chain.
6 Had Della known that Jim was going to buy the combs, would she have cut her hair?

Fronting as a literary device

The standard, basic word order of sentences in English is subject + verb + object. When we change the order of these – and, for example, start a sentence with an object – it is called 'fronting'. This is fairly common in both informal speech and in writing. It is used throughout *The Gift of the Magi* as a literary device.

Look at the pair of sentences below. Notice the change in the word order.

Normal word order: *Della counted it three times.*
Word order with fronting: *Three times Della counted it.* (The emphasis is on the number of times she counted.)

Inversion after fronting

Sometimes the subject and verb are inverted after fronting. This is usually when the fronted sentence would finish with a verb if there was no inversion.

Look at the example below.

Normal word order: *The watch was grand.*
Fronting without inversion: *Grand the watch was.* (More common in speech.)
Fronting with inversion: *Grand was the watch.* (More literary.)

9 Rewrite these fronted sentences with normal word order. What is the difference in the effect?

1 On went her old brown jacket; on went her old brown hat.
2 One flight up Della ran.
3 Down rippled the brown cascade.
4 Twenty-one dollars they took from her for it.
5 Out of his trance Jim seemed quickly to wake.

Literary analysis
Plot
1 Number the events in the story in the order in which they happen.
   a) Della showed Jim his present from her
   b) Jim showed Della her present from him
   c) Della decided to sell her hair
   d) Jim came home
   e) Jim told Della he had sold his watch
   f) Jim realised Della had cut her hair
   g) Della counted the money she had saved
2 When did Jim sell his watch? When did he buy the combs? Is it important to know exactly when these things happened? Why/why not?
3 O Henry's stories are famous for their surprise endings. What exactly is the surprise in this story? Did you guess that Jim had sold his watch? If yes, when did you first realise that Della's gift was going to be useless?
4 What was the *gift of the magi*? What did the couple have that was far more important than the gifts they had bought each other?

Characters
5 Three other characters appear in the story. Who are they? Who do we know most about? Who do we know least about? Why?
6 The author describes Della through her actions and her reactions. What picture do we form of her? Choose three adjectives to describe her. Which actions or reactions influenced your choice?
7 What adjectives does O Henry use to describe Jim? Are these adjectives mirrored in his actions?
8 What impression do you get of Madame Sofronie? How does the author create this impression?
9 Think of the gifts Jim and Della choose for each other and the sacrifices they make. What does this tell us about them?
10 The author refers to the characters as *two foolish children*. In what way are they foolish? In what way are they children? Do you think this description is fair?

Narration

11 The story is told in the third person. What adjectives would you choose to describe the voice of the narrator?
12 How do you think the story would have been told differently if the narrator had been (a) Della; (b) Jim?
13 The narrator often talks directly to the reader to comment on the scene or the action as if both he and the readers were present in the flat. What effect does this have?
14 The narrator sometimes interrupts the story to make philosophical comments on life. What effect does this have?
15 What exactly is the narrator telling us in the last paragraph?

Style

16 Look at the opening paragraph. Notice how many times the money is referred to. Notice the repetition of the word *pennies*. What effect does this have?
17 What other details does the author describe in the next few paragraphs to underline the couple's poverty?
18 Notice the descriptions of the letterbox and the electric button. Notice how the structure is repeated. What effect does this have?
19 The author makes frequent use of repetition in the story. Look at the examples below. Underline the words that are repeated. What is being emphasised by the repetition in each example?
    1 *She stood by the window and looked out dully at a gray cat walking a gray fence in a gray backyard* [page 19].
    2 *On went her old brown jacket; on went her old brown hat* [page 20].
    3 *O all who give and receive gifts, such as they are wisest. Everywhere they are wisest. They are the magi* [page 24].
20 Notice the words in bold that are used to describe Della when she leaves the house to sell her hair and buy a present.

    *With a **whirl** of skirts and with the brilliant **sparkle** still in her eyes, she **fluttered** out the door and down the stairs to the street* [page 20].

    *The next two hours **tripped** by on rosy wings* [page 20].

    What is Della being compared to? What does this tell us about her mood and her attitude?
21 Notice the description of Della's hair. What does the author compare it to? What qualities does the comparison emphasise? What effect does the comparison have?

22 Look at the passage that describes the scene when Della sells her hair [page 20]. Notice the use of direct speech and the short sentences and exchanges. What does this tell us about the act of selling her hair? In what way is it in contrast with the importance of Della's decision?
23 Look at the other examples of direct speech in the story. What is the effect each time?
24 Notice the use of capitals in referring to *The Watch* and *The Combs*. Why does the author use capitals? What is being suggested?
25 Look at the narrator's comment about the importance of money when Jim first hugs his wife when he gets home. In what way does this comment suggest the surprise at the end of the story?
26 Think of the style and tone of the story as a whole. Which of the following adjectives would you use to describe it? Why?

> clever   dramatic   humorous   melodramatic[47]   moral
> sentimental[48]   simplistic[49]

Guidance to the above literary terms, answer keys to all the exercises and activities, plus a wealth of other reading-practice material, can be found on the student's section of the Macmillan Readers website at: www.macmillanenglish.com/readers.

---

47 too emotional or too serious
48 emphasising emotions
49 treating something in a way that makes it seem much more simple than it really is

The Lost Phœbe
by Theodore Dreiser

About the author

Theodore Dreiser was born in 1871 in Terre Haute, Indiana, in the Middle West of the USA. His family was very poor and very large – Dreiser was the ninth of ten surviving children. His father, a Catholic German immigrant, was very strict. In the 1860s, the family's woollen mill[1] was destroyed by fire. After that, they moved from town to town as Dreiser's father looked for work.

Dreiser left home when he was 16 and did a variety of jobs. Then, a sympathetic ex-teacher who saw his talent helped him to get a place at Indiana University. However, Dreiser did not enjoy academic life and left after just one year. He then worked as a journalist for three years in Chicago. In 1894 ,he moved to New York City, where he worked as a journalist for various newspapers and magazines.

In 1898, Dreiser married Sara White, a school teacher from Missouri, but the marriage was not a happy one. They separated in 1909. After his wife's death in 1942, Dreiser married his cousin Helen, who had been his companion since 1919. Their marriage was not always easy but Helen stayed with Dreiser until his death in 1945.

Dreiser's first novel was *Sister Carrie* (1900), the story of a young working girl. The publishers did not approve of the book because it did not follow established morals – 'bad' characters were not punished and vice[2] was rewarded. As a result, Dreiser had to make a lot of revisions to the story in order to get it published. The book was not given much publicity and few copies were sold. However, the novel was republished in 1907 and it became one of the most famous urban novels in literary history. Dreiser's original unrevised version of *Sister Carrie* was not published until 1981.

Dreiser was very depressed by the poor commercial success of his book and the attempts to censor[3] it. He worked as an editor for several

---

1 a building where wool is manufactured
2 *formal:* extremely bad and immoral behaviour
3 to remove parts of a book, film, letter etc for moral, religious or political reasons

women's magazines, and ten years passed before the publication of his next novel, *Jennie Gerhardt*. Like *Sister Carrie*, it was attacked for its realism. In the story, a young, unmarried woman, Jennie, is seduced by a senator[4] and has a baby. Again, the publishers censored parts of the book.

Between 1911 and 1925, Dreiser had 14 books published. In 1912, he travelled to Europe and wrote about his experiences in *A Traveller at Forty* (1913). In the 1920s, he travelled across Russia and described his experiences in *Dreiser Looks at Russia* (1928). His concern for the ordinary man and his hatred of poverty gave him some sympathy for communism. He finally joined the Communist Party five months before his death. At this time, he talked of his 'belief in the greatness and dignity of man'.

Dreiser's most commercially successful book was *An American Tragedy* (1925). It was based on a real murder case which had fascinated Dreiser for years. Two film versions were made of the book, the first in 1931 and the second, *A Place in the Sun*, in 1951. Dreiser finally made some money from his writing and his circumstances improved. He was able to move into a better apartment and build a house in the country.

Dreiser left New York in 1938 and settled permanently in California. The same year, he travelled for the last time to New York to receive the Award of Merit from the American Academy of Arts and Letters. They cited *Sister Carrie*, *Twelve Men*, and *An American Tragedy* as his greatest works.

When Dreiser died in December 1945, he was still writing. His last book, *The Stoic*, was published after his death. He was one of the greatest naturalist[5] writers in American literature and a strong defender of freedom of expression.

About the story

The Lost Phœbe first appeared in *The Century Magazine*, April 1916. In 1918, it was included in Dreiser's first collection of short stories, *Free and Other Stories*.

---

4 a member of the senate, the more senior part of the US Congress or parliament
5 writers of the naturalist school were interested in portraying reality and in the importance of environment and heredity in determining character

Background information

The Midwest

The story is set in the Midwest (or Middle West) of the USA where Dreiser grew up. The Midwest covers several states between the Ohio River and the Rocky Mountains. It was colonised by European immigrants in the 19th century. Many immigrants came from rural backgrounds and became farmers in their new country. In the first part of the 20th century, the population of the towns decreased as people travelled to the larger cities to work in industry. Chicago, where Dreiser worked, was the biggest city in the Midwest.

In the story, Henry and Phœbe live on a run-down, isolated farm. We are told that there is *perhaps a house every other mile or so*.

Immigration

The surname of the protagonists (Reifsneider) is German, which suggests that they are from a family of German immigrants. Dreiser's own father was German.

In the second half of the 19th century, 30 million people emigrated to the USA from around the world. Emigration from Germany was especially popular – in 1890 the USA had 800 German newspapers.

Religion

The immigrants brought with them a variety of religions. Dreiser's father was a strict Roman Catholic and his mother was from a Mennonite[6] family from Pennsylvania. Because of religious tensions, the young couple had to run away in order to get married.

The protagonists of the story are *moderately Christian*. They do not seem to attend church. Henry reads the Bible after Phœbe's death but finds little comfort in it.

---

6 the Mennonite church is a Protestant church which originated in Holland in the 16th century

Summary

It may help you to know something about what happens in the story before you read it. Don't worry, this summary does *not* tell you how the story ends!

The story takes place in the Midwest of the USA in the early years of the 20th century. An old, married couple, Henry and Phœbe Reifsneider, live in a farming area that is in decline. Their children have all left home and their lives are simple and full of familiar routine, unaffected by the outside world. When Phœbe dies after a short illness, Henry is left alone in the old house where he has lived all his married life. He refuses invitations to go and live with his children and tries to continue to live in the same way as before.

He misses Phœbe and spends a lot of time thinking about her. One night he imagines that he sees her in the house. He then thinks he sees her on several more occasions.

Henry convinces himself that Phœbe has left him after an argument, as she sometimes jokingly said she would when she was alive. Eventually he sets out to look for Phœbe. He asks a farmer on the road if he has seen her. He then visits a neighbour and asks her the same thing. These people realise that Henry is losing his mind.

The years pass and Henry continues his search for his missing wife. He is not thought to be a danger to society and is allowed to wander freely around the countryside. He neglects his house and his appearance and spends most of his time searching for Phœbe. He becomes a familiar figure walking around the area for miles every day and sometimes sleeping outdoors.

One spring night, seven years after Phœbe's death, Henry becomes convinced that he is soon to see his wife and speak to her once more.

Pre-reading exercises

Key vocabulary

This section will help you familiarise yourself with some of the more specific vocabulary used in the story. You may want to use it to help you before you start reading, or as a revision exercise after you have finished the story.

Words for describing old age and neglect

In the story, Henry and Phœbe's house and its surroundings are described in detail. The building and its furniture are old and neglected.

1 **Look at the words and phrases in the left-hand column below and match them with the correct definitions in the right-hand column.**

1	**faded-looking**	a)	old and twisted and covered in lines
2	**musty**	b)	too old or too old-fashioned to be useful
3	**worm-eaten**	c)	old and no longer in good condition
4	**lime-stained**	d)	something looks like this when its colour gradually becomes pale
5	**decrepit**	e)	smelling unpleasant and not fresh
6	**antiquated**	f)	full of holes made by worms
7	**gnarled**	g)	with marks made by a white substance that is used for making cement and helping plants to grow
8	**spongy**	h)	if something does this, liquid or gas comes out of it through a hole or a crack
9	**leak**	i)	with a surface that sinks when you push it, then returns to its original shape

2 **Complete these sentences with the correct form of the words and expressions above.**

1 When it rains, the roof .... and leaves pools of water on the floor.
2 Those curtains used to be a much darker colour but they are .... now from the sun.
3 The attic has been closed for years and it smells very ....
4 The wooden chest is useful but you can see from all the holes in it that it is ....
5 Record players are now rather .... ; few people buy records these days.

6 The grass in the garden was soft and .... from the rain.
7 The house is totally ....; we might as well knock it down and build a new one.
8 That table has been outside and is very ....; perhaps we can remove the marks with something.
9 I love the shapes of the old, ... branches on the apple trees.

Henry

3 These words are used to describe Henry. Match them with their meanings and then complete the paragraph.

1 **crotchety**   a) a face with a lot of lines on it
2 **crows' feet** b) physically weak, especially when you are old and sick
3 **straggling**   c) someone who is easily annoyed
4 **feeble**   d) wrinkles in the skin at the corners of your eyes
5 **seamed**   e) growing in a messy way

After Phœbe's death, Henry became even more bad-tempered and (1) .... than before. His began to neglect his appearance: his hair and beard grew long and (2) .... His face was lined, especially his brow which was burnt and (3) .... from the sun. Around his eyes, the (4) .... resembled lines on a map. As the years passed, Henry grew thinner and more (5) ...., from walking too much and eating too little.

Spoken language

The people in the story are farmers from the US Midwest. Dreiser tries to portray their accent and the non-standard features of their speech.

4 Look at this conversation between Phœbe and Henry. Try reading it to yourself or with another person. Is the meaning clear?

"Phœbe, where's my corn knife? You ain't never minded to let my things alone no more."

"Now you hush[7], Henry," his wife would caution him in a cracked and squeaky voice. "If you don't, I'll leave yuh. I'll git up and walk out of here some day, and then where would y' be? Y' aint got anybody but me to look after yuh, so yuh just behave yourself. Your corn knife's on

---

7 a way of telling someone to be quiet

the mantel where it's allus been unless you've gone an' put it summers else."

5 Now try to answer the questions below about the extract.
1 *Ain't* appears twice in the conversation with different meanings. What are they?
2 What is the meaning of the second sentence?
3 How is the word 'you' represented?
4 What do these words mean in the extract: *git; allus; summers*?

6 This is what Henry says to Dr Morrow after Phœbe dies. How would you write his words in standard English?

"I kin make a shift for myself ... I kin cook a little."

Main themes

Before you read the story, you may want to think about some of its main themes. The questions will help you think about the story as you're reading it for the first time. There is more discussion of the main themes in the *Literary analysis* section after the story.

Marriage

A particular type of marriage is described in the story. Henry and Phœbe have lived together for many years and have come to depend on each other. Henry, in particular, is very dependent on his wife. They are poor, but reasonably content with their routines, and the tasks of the small farm. Their children live far away and the couple have little communication with them. They have neighbours, but must make an effort to see them because they live some distance away. Their world is reduced to their orchard, fields and animals. When Phœbe dies, Henry feels lost and alone.

Grief and madness

Dreiser paints a very vivid picture of how an ordinary man gradually loses his mind through grief and isolation. At first, Henry tries to continue his life as before, but it loses its meaning because of his wife's absence. His activities become fewer and he starts to neglect everything. Then, he begins to 'see' Phœbe and dreams about her. He imagines that Phœbe has run away and he must look for her. Sympathetic neighbours realise what has happened and soon he becomes a familiar figure, wandering around the countryside. He starts to sleep outside and begins to call out for Phœbe. He imagines that she is guiding him towards her. Finally, one night, he wakes and sees her and runs eagerly after her.

★ ★ ★ ★

The Lost Phœbe

by Theodore Dreiser

They lived together in a part of the country which was not so prosperous as it had once been, about three miles from one of those small towns that, instead of increasing in population, is steadily decreasing. The territory was not very thickly settled[8]; perhaps a house every other mile or so, with large areas of corn- and wheat-land and **fallow** fields that at odd seasons had been sown to timothy[9] and clover[10]. Their particular house was part **log** and part frame, the log portion being the old original home of Henry's grandfather. The new portion, of now rain-beaten, time-worn **slabs**, through which the wind **squeaked** in **chinks** at times, and which several overshadowing elms[11] and a butternut-tree made picturesque and **reminiscently** pathetic, but a little damp, was erected by Henry when he was twenty-one and just married.

That was forty-eight years before. The furniture inside, like the house outside, was old and mildewy[12] and reminiscent of an earlier day. You have seen the what-not[13] of cherry wood, perhaps, with spiral legs[14] and fluted[15] top. It was there. The old-fashioned **four poster** bed, with its ball-like protuberances and deep curving incisions, was there also, a sadly alienated descendant of an early Jacobean[16] ancestor. The bureau[17] of cherry was also high and wide and solidly built, but faded-

8 populated
9 a type of grass used to feed animals
10 a small plant with leaves that have three round parts
11 a large tree with round leaves that fall off in winter
12 (usually *mildewed*) covered with a fungus like a white powder
13 *old fashioned*: a piece of furniture with shelves for displaying plants and ornaments
14 *phrase 'spiral legs'*: legs that have a twisted pattern
15 decorated with long, deep parallel lines
16 typical of the period 1603–1625 when James I was king of England
17 piece of furniture with several drawers for holding things such as clothes or towels

looking, and with a musty odor. The rag carpet that underlay[18] all these **sturdy** examples of enduring furniture was a weak, faded, lead-and-pink-colored affair woven by Phœbe Ann's own hands, when she was fifteen years younger than she was when she died. The **creaky** wooden **loom** on which it had been done now stood like a dusty, bony skeleton, along with a broken **rocking-chair**, a worm-eaten **clothes-press** – Heaven knows how old – a lime-stained bench that had once been used to keep flowers on outside the door, and other decrepit factors of household utility, in an east room that was a lean-to[19] against this so-called main portion. All sorts of other broken-down furniture were about this place; an antiquated **clothes-horse**, cracked in two of its ribs; a broken mirror in an old cherry frame, which had fallen from a nail and cracked itself three days before their youngest son, Jerry, died; an extension hat-rack, which once had had porcelain knobs on the ends of its pegs; and a sewing-machine, long since outdone[20] in its clumsy mechanism by rivals of a newer generation.

The **orchard** to the east of the house was full of gnarled old apple-trees, worm-eaten as to[21] trunks and branches, and fully ornamented with green and white **lichens**, so that it had a sad, greenish-white, silvery effect in moonlight. The low **outhouses**, which had once housed chickens, a horse or two, a cow, and several pigs, were covered with patches of **moss** as to their roof, and the sides had been free of paint for so long that they were blackish gray as to color, and a little spongy. The picket-fence[22] in front, with its gate squeaky and askew[23], and the side fences of the stake-and-rider[24] type were in an equally run-down[25] condition. As a matter of fact, they had aged synchronously[26]

18 *unusual*: lay under
19 a building that shares a wall with a larger building and has a roof that leans against that wall
20 *unusual*: made to look old-fashioned
21 *unusual*: in the part or area of something
22 a fence made of thin, flat boards that are pointed at the top
23 at an angle instead of straight
24 a fence made with crossed *stakes* supporting horizontal rails, or *riders*
25 in bad condition
26 *unusual, technical*: at the same time as

with the persons who lived here, old Henry Reifsneider and his wife Phœbe Ann.

They had lived here, these two, ever since their marriage, forty-eight years before, and Henry had lived here before that from his childhood up. His father and mother, well along in years[27] when he was a boy, had invited him to bring his wife here when he had first fallen in love and decided to marry; and he had done so. His father and mother were the companions of himself and his wife for ten years after they were married, when both died; and then Henry and Phœbe were left with their five children growing lustily apace[28]. But all sorts of things had happened since then. Of the seven children, all told[29], that had been born to them, three had died; one girl had gone to Kansas; one boy had gone to Sioux Falls, never even to be heard of after; another boy had gone to Washington; and the last girl lived five counties away in the same State, but was so burdened with cares of her own that she rarely gave them a thought. Time and a **commonplace** home life that had never been attractive had **weaned** them thoroughly, so that, wherever they were, they gave little thought as to how it might be with their father and mother.

Old Henry Reifsneider and his wife Phœbe were a loving couple. You perhaps know how it is with simple natures that fasten themselves like lichens on the stones of circumstance and **weather** their days to a **crumbling** conclusion. The great world sounds[30] widely, but it has no call for them. They have no soaring intellect. The orchard, the meadow, the corn-field, the pig-pen[31], and the chicken-lot[32] measure the range of their human activities. When the wheat is headed[33] it is reaped and threshed; when the corn is browned and frosted it is cut and shocked[34]; when the timothy is in full head it is cut, and the

27 *phrase 'well along in years'*: getting old
28 very quickly
29 *phrase 'all told'*: in total
30 intransitive verb meaning *makes itself heard*
31 a small building on a farm where pigs are kept
32 a lot is a small area of land
33 fully grown
34 made into 'shocks' or groups of sheaves of grain, placed on end and supporting one another in a field

hay-cock[35] erected. After that comes winter, with the **hauling** of grain to market, the sawing and splitting of wood, the simple chores of fire-building, meal-getting, occasional repairing, and visiting. Beyond these and the changes of weather – the snow, the rains, and the fair days – there are no immediate, significant things. All the rest of life is a far-off, clamorous phantasmagoria[36], **flickering** like Northern lights[37] in the night, and sounding as faintly as cow-bells tinkling in the distance.

Old Henry and his wife Phœbe were as fond of each other as it is possible for two old people to be who have nothing else in this life to be fond of. He was a thin old man, seventy when she died, a queer, crotchety person with coarse gray-black hair and beard, quite straggly and **unkempt**. He looked at you out of dull, fishy, watery eyes that had deep-brown crows'-feet at the sides. His clothes, like the clothes of many farmers, were aged and angular and **baggy**, standing out at the pockets, not fitting around the neck, **protuberant** and worn at elbow and knee. Phœbe Ann was thin and shapeless, a very umbrella of a woman, clad[38] in shabby black, and with a black bonnet for her best wear. As time had passed, and they had only themselves to look after, their movements had become slower and slower, their activities fewer and fewer. The annual keep[39] of pigs had been reduced from five to one grunting porker[40], and the single horse which Henry now retained was a sleepy animal, not over-nourished and not very clean. The chickens, of which formerly there was a large flock, had almost disappeared, owing to **ferrets**, foxes, and the lack of proper care, which produces disease. The former healthy garden was now a straggling memory of itself, and the vines and flower-beds that formerly ornamented the windows and dooryard had now become choking thickets[41]. A **will** had been made which

---

35 a large pile of hay in a field that has been built up and cut in order to store it
36 *unusual*: a scene that is like something you see in a dream
37 colourful bands of lights that you sometimes see in the sky in northern parts of the world
38 *mainly literary*: dressed in
39 number
40 a young pig that has been made fat so that it can be eaten
41 an area with a lot of bushes and small trees growing very close together

divided the small tax-eaten property equally among the remaining four, so that it was really of no interest to any of them. Yet these two lived together in peace and sympathy, only that now and then old Henry would become unduly[42] cranky[43], complaining almost invariably that something had been neglected or **mislaid** which was of no importance at all.

"Phœbe, where's my corn-knife? You ain't never minded to let my things alone no more."

"Now you hush, Henry," his wife would caution him in a cracked and squeaky voice. "If you don't, I'll leave yuh. I'll git up and walk out of here some day, and then where would y' be? Y' ain't got anybody but me to look after yuh, so yuh just behave yourself. Your corn-knife's on the mantel[44] where it's allus been unless you've gone an' put it summers else."

Old Henry, who knew his wife would never leave him in any circumstances, used to speculate at times as to what he would do if she were to die. That was the one leaving that he really feared. As he climbed on the chair at night to **wind** the old, long-pendulumed, double-weighted clock, or went finally to the front and the back door to see that they were safely shut in, it was a comfort to know that Phœbe was there, properly ensconced[45] on her side of the bed, and that if he stirred restlessly in the night, she would be there to ask what he wanted.

"Now, Henry, do lie still! You're as restless as a chicken."

"Well, I can't sleep, Phœbe."

"Well, yuh needn't roll so, anyhow. Yuh kin let me sleep."

This usually reduced him to a state of somnolent[46] ease. If she wanted a pail of water, it was a **grumbling** pleasure for him to get it; and if she did rise first to build the fires, he saw that the wood was cut and placed within easy reach. They divided this simple world nicely between them.

As the years had gone on, however, fewer and fewer people had called. They were well-known for a distance of as much

42 *formal:* to a greater degree than is reasonable or necessary
43 *informal:* irritable, easily annoyed
44 a shelf above the opening of a fireplace
45 *mainly literary:* in a safe or comfortable position
46 *formal:* feeling ready to sleep

as ten square miles as old Mr. and Mrs. Reifsneider, honest, moderately Christian, but too old to be really interesting any longer. The writing of letters had become an almost impossible burden too difficult to continue or even negotiate via others, although an occasional letter still did arrive from the daughter in Pemberton County. Now and then some old friend stopped with a pie or cake or a roasted chicken or duck, or merely to see that they were well; but even these kindly minded visits were no longer frequent.

One day in the early spring of her sixty-fourth year Mrs. Reifsneider took sick[47], and from a low fever passed into some indefinable ailment[48] which, because of her age, was no longer curable. Old Henry drove to Swinnerton, the neighboring town, and procured[49] a doctor. Some friends called, and the immediate care of her was taken off his hands. Then one **chill** spring night she died, and old Henry, in a fog of **sorrow** and uncertainty, followed her body to the nearest graveyard, an unattractive space with a few pines growing in it. Although he might have gone to the daughter in Pemberton or sent for her, it was really too much trouble and he was too **weary** and fixed[50]. It was suggested to him at once by one friend and another that he come to stay with them awhile[51], but he did not see fit[52]. He was so old and so fixed in his notions and so accustomed to the exact surroundings he had known all his days, that he could not think of leaving. He wanted to remain near where they had put his Phœbe; and the fact that he would have to live alone did not trouble him in the least. The living children were notified and the care of him offered if he would leave, but he would not.

"I kin make a shift for myself," he continually announced to old Dr. Morrow, who had attended his wife in this case. "I kin cook a little, and, besides, it don't take much more'n coffee an' bread

47 *phrase 'took sick'*: became ill
48 an illness, usually not a serious one
49 *formal*: obtained something with effort or difficulty
50 used to doing something in a certain way
51 for a while
52 *phrase 'see fit'*: to consider something to be right or suitable (to do)

in the mornin's to satisfy me. I'll get along now well enough. Yuh just let me be." And after many **pleadings** and proffers[53] of advice, with supplies of coffee and bacon and baked bread **duly** offered and accepted, he was left to himself. For a while he sat **idly** outside his door **brooding** in the spring sun. He tried to revive his interest in farming, and to keep himself busy and free from thought by looking after the fields, which of late had been much neglected. It was a **gloomy** thing to come in of an evening, however, or in the afternoon and find no shadow of Phœbe where everything suggested her. By degrees he put a few of her things away. At night he sat beside his lamp and read in the papers that were left him occasionally or in a Bible that he had neglected for years, but he could get little **solace** from these things. Mostly he held his hand over his mouth and looked at the floor as he sat and thought of what had become of her, and how soon he himself would die. He made a great business of making his coffee in the morning and frying himself a little bacon at night; but his appetite was gone. The shell in which he had been housed so long seemed vacant, and its shadows were suggestive of immedicable[54] griefs. So he lived quite **dolefully** for five long months, and then a change began.

It was one night, after he had looked after the front and back door, wound the clock, blown out the light, and gone through all the selfsame[55] motions that he had indulged in for years, that he went to bed not so much to sleep as to think. It was a moonlight night. The green-lichen-covered orchard just outside and to be seen from his bed where he now lay was a silvery affair, sweetly **spectral**. The moon shone through the east windows, throwing the pattern of the panes on the wooden floor, and making the old furniture, to which he was accustomed, stand out dimly in the room. As usual he had been thinking of Phœbe and the years when they had been young together, and of the children who had gone, and the poor shift he was making of his present days. The house was coming to be in a very bad state indeed.

53 offers
54 *unusual*: not made better by medicine
55 same, familiar

The bed-clothes were in disorder and not clean, for he made a **wretched** shift of washing. It was a terror to him. The roof leaked, causing things, some of them, to remain damp for weeks at a time, but he was getting into that brooding state where he would accept anything rather than exert himself. He preferred to pace[56] slowly to and fro or to sit and think.

By twelve o'clock of this particular night he was asleep, however, and by two had waked again. The moon by this time had shifted to a position on the western side of the house, and it now shone in through the windows of the living-room and those of the kitchen beyond. A certain combination of furniture – a chair near a table, with his coat on it, the half-open kitchen door casting a shadow, and the position of a lamp near a paper – gave him an exact representation of Phœbe leaning over the table as he had often seen her do in life. It gave him a great start[57]. Could it be she – or her ghost? He had scarcely ever believed in spirits; and still – He looked at her fixedly in the **feeble** half-light, his old hair **tingling** oddly at the roots, and then sat up. The figure did not move. He put his thin legs out of the bed and sat looking at her, wondering if this could really be Phœbe. They had talked of ghosts often in their lifetime, of **apparitions** and **omens**; but they had never agreed that such things could be. It had never been a part of his wife's **creed** that she could have a spirit that could return to walk the earth. Her after-world[58] was quite a different affair, a vague heaven, no less, from which the righteous did not trouble to return. Yet here she was now, bending over the table in her black skirt and gray shawl, her pale profile outlined against the moonlight.

"Phœbe," he called, **thrilling** from head to toe and putting out one bony hand, "have yuh come back?"

The figure did not stir, and he arose and walked uncertainly to the door, looking at it fixedly the while. As he drew near, however, the apparition resolved itself into its primal[59] content

---

56 to walk with slow, steady steps, especially when you are anxious about something
57 shock
58 place where you go after you die
59 original

– his old coat over the high-backed chair, the lamp by the paper, the half-open door.

"Well," he said to himself, his mouth open, "I thought shore[60] I saw her." And he ran his hand strangely and vaguely through his hair, the while[61] his nervous tension relaxed. Vanished as it had, it gave him the idea that she might return.

Another night, because of this first illusion, and because his mind was now constantly on her and he was old, he looked out of the window that was nearest his bed and commanded[62] a hen-coop and pig-pen and a part of the wagon-shed, and there, a faint mist exuding from the damp of the ground, he thought he saw her again. It was one of those little **wisps** of mist, one of those faint exhalations[63] of the earth that rise in a cool night after a warm day, and flicker like small white cypresses[64] of fog before they disappear. In life it had been a custom of hers to cross this lot from her kitchen door to the pig-pen to throw in any scrap that was left from her cooking, and here she was again. He sat up and watched it strangely, doubtfully, because of his previous experience, but inclined, because of the nervous titillation[65] that passed over his body, to believe that spirits really were, and that Phœbe, who would be concerned because of his lonely state, must be thinking about him, and hence[66] returning. What other way would she have? How otherwise could she express herself? It would be within the province of her charity so to do, and like her loving interest in him. He **quivered** and watched it eagerly; but, a faint breath of air stirring, it wound away toward the fence and disappeared.

A third night, as he was actually dreaming, some ten days later, she came to his bedside and put her hand on his head.

"Poor Henry!" she said. "It's too bad."

He **roused** out of his sleep, actually to see her, he thought, moving from his bed-room into the one living-room, her figure

60 sure
61 *phrase 'the while'*: while
62 had a view of, overlooked
63 breathing out through your mouth and nose
64 a tall tree with dark green leaves that do not fall off in winter
65 a feeling of interest, pleasure or excitement
66 therefore

a shadowy mass of black. The weak **straining** of his eyes caused little points of light to flicker about the outlines of her form. He arose[67], greatly astonished, walked the floor in the cool room, convinced that Phœbe was coming back to him. If he only thought sufficiently, if he made it perfectly clear by his feeling that he needed her greatly, she would come back, this kindly wife, and tell him what to do. She would perhaps be with him much of the time, in the night, anyhow; and that would make him less lonely, this state more **endurable**.

In age and with the feeble it is not such a far cry from the subtleties of illusion[68] to actual hallucination[69], and in due time this transition was made for Henry. Night after night he waited, expecting her return. Once in his **weird** mood he thought he saw a pale light moving about the room, and another time he thought he saw her walking in the orchard after dark. It was one morning when the details of his lonely state were virtually unendurable that he woke with the thought that she was not dead. How he had arrived at this conclusion it is hard to say. His mind had gone. In its place was a fixed illusion. He and Phœbe had had a senseless quarrel. He had **reproached** her for not leaving his pipe where he was accustomed to find it, and she had left. It was an aberrated[70] **fulfilment** of her old **jesting** threat that if he did not behave himself she would leave him.

"I guess I could find yuh ag'in," he had always said. But her crackling[71] threat had always been:

"Yuh'll not find me if I ever leave yuh. I guess I kin git some place where yuh can't find me."

This morning when he arose he did not think to build the fire in the customary way or to grind his coffee and cut his bread, as was his wont[72], but solely to meditate as to where he should

---

67 *literary*: got up out of bed
68 an appearance or effect that is different from the way things really are
69 something that you think you can see or hear, but that is not really there, caused by an illness or the effect of drugs
70 (more usual, *aberrant*) not normal or not what you would usually expect
71 teasing or lively
72 to be in the habit of doing a particular thing

search for her and how he should induce[73] her to come back. Recently the one horse had been dispensed with[74] because he found it **cumbersome** and beyond his needs. He took down his soft crush hat[75] after he had dressed himself, a new **glint** of interest and determination in his eye, and taking his black **crook cane** from behind the door, where he had always placed it, started out **briskly** to look for her among the nearest neighbors. His old shoes clumped soundly in the dust as he walked, and his gray-black locks[76], now grown rather long, straggled out in a dramatic fringe or **halo** from under his hat. His short coat stirred busily as he walked, and his hands and face were peaked[77] and pale.

"Why, hello, Henry! Where're yuh goin' this morning?" inquired Farmer Dodge, who, hauling a load of wheat to market, encountered[78] him on the public road. He had not seen the aged farmer in months, not since his wife's death, and he wondered now, seeing him looking so spry[79].

"Yuh ain't seen Phœbe, have yuh?" inquired the old man, looking up quizzically[80].

"Phœbe who?" inquired Farmer Dodge, not for the moment connecting the name with Henry's dead wife.

"Why, my wife Phœbe, o' course. Who do yuh s'pose I mean?" He stared up with a pathetic sharpness of glance from under his **shaggy**, gray eyebrows.

"Wall, I'll swan[81], Henry, yuh ain't jokin', are yuh?" said the solid Dodge, a pursy[82] man, with a smooth, hard, red face. "It can't be your wife yuh're talkin' about. She's dead."

73 persuade
74 *formal*: to no longer use someone or something because you no longer want or need them
75 a soft hat
76 *literary*: a small piece of hair from someone's head
77 pale and sickly in appearance
78 *formal*: to meet someone
79 *of an old person*: still very healthy and energetic
80 showing that you are confused or surprised by something and perhaps thinking it is rather strange and funny
81 *US*: exclamation of surprise
82 (more usual: *pursed*) when you purse your lips, you press them together and outward because you are angry or thinking

"Dead! Shucks[83]!" **retorted** the **demented** Reifsneider. "She left me early this mornin', while I was sleepin'. She allus got up to build the fire, but she's gone now. We had a little spat[84] last night, an' I guess that's the reason. But I guess I kin find her. She's gone over to Matilda Race's; that's where she's gone."

He started briskly up the road, leaving the amazed Dodge to stare in wonder after him.

"Well, I'll be switched[85]!" he said aloud to himself. "He's clean out'n his head. That poor feller's been livin' down there till he's gone outen his mind. I'll have to notify the authorities." And he **flicked** his **whip** with great enthusiasm. "Geddap!" he said, and was off.

Reifsneider met no one else in this poorly populated region until he reached the whitewashed fence of Matilda Race and her husband three miles away. He had passed several other houses en route[86], but these not being within the range of his illusion were not considered. His wife, who had known Matilda well, must be here. He opened the picket-gate which guarded the walk, and **stamped** briskly up to the door.

"Why, Mr. Reifsneider," exclaimed old Matilda herself, a **stout** woman, looking out of the door in answer to his knock, "what brings yuh here this mornin'?"

"Is Phœbe here?" he demanded eagerly.

"Phœbe who? What Phœbe?" replied Mrs. Race, curious as to this sudden development of energy on his part.

"Why, my Phœbe, o' course. My wife Phœbe. Who do yuh s'pose? Ain't she here now?"

"Lawsy me[87]!" exclaimed Ms. Race, opening her mouth. "Yuh pore man! So you're clean out'n your mind now. Yuh come right in and sit down. I'll git yuh a cup o' coffee. O' course your wife ain't here, but yuh come in an' sit down. I'll find her fer yuh after a while. I know where she is."

83 US: an interjection used to express disappointment, bashfulness or irritation
84 a short argument
85 US: exclamation expressing surprise
86 *French, phrase 'en route'*: on the way
87 US: exclamation, perhaps a corruption of 'Lord'

The old farmer's eyes softened, and he entered. He was so thin and pale a specimen, pantalooned[88] and patriarchal[89], that he **aroused** Mrs. Race's extremest sympathy as he took off his hat and laid it on his knees quite softly and mildly.

"We had a quarrel last night, an' she left me," he volunteered.

"Laws! laws!" sighed Mrs. Race, there being no one present with whom to share her astonishment as she went to her kitchen. "The pore man! Now somebody's just got to look after him. He can't be allowed to run around the country this way lookin' for his dead wife. It's terrible."

She boiled him a pot of coffee and brought in some of her new-baked bread and fresh butter. She set out some of her best jam and put a couple of eggs to boil, lying whole-heartedly[90] the while.

"Now yuh stay right there, Uncle Henry, till Jake comes in, an' I'll send him to look for Phœbe. I think it's more likely she's over to Swinnerton with some o' her friends. Anyhow, we'll find out. Now yuh just drink this coffee an' eat this bread. Yuh must be tired. Yuh've had a long walk this mornin'." Her idea was to take counsel with Jake, "her man", and perhaps have him notify the authorities.

She **bustled** about, meditating on the uncertainties of life, while old Reifsneider thrummed[91] on the rim of his hat with his pale fingers and later ate abstractedly of what she offered. His mind was on his wife, however, and since she was not here, or did not appear, it wandered vaguely away to a family the name of Murray, miles away in another direction. He decided after a time that he would not wait for Jake Race to hunt his wife but would seek[92] her for himself. He must be on[93], and urge her to come back.

88 *old-fashioned*: long, wide trousers that become narrower
89 a patriarchal society is one in which men have all or most of the power
90 enthusiastically, completely
91 to make a low, regular noise like one object gently hitting another many times
92 *formal*: to ask for something or try to get something
93 to continue a journey

"Well, I'll be goin'," he said, getting up and looking strangely about him. "I guess she didn't come here after all. She went over to the Murrays', I guess. I'll not wait any longer, Mis' Race. There's a lot to do over to the house to-day." And out he marched in the face of her protests taking to[94] the dusty road again in the warm spring sun, his cane striking the earth as he went.

It was two hours later that this pale figure of a man appeared in the Murrays' doorway, dusty, **perspiring**, eager. He had **tramped** all of five miles, and it was noon. An amazed husband and wife of sixty heard his strange **query**, and realized also that he was mad. They begged him to stay to dinner, intending to notify the authorities later and see what could be done, but though he stayed to partake of[95] a little something, he did not stay long, and was off again to another distant farmhouse, his idea of many things to do and his need of Phœbe impelling[96] him. So it went for that day and the next, the circle of his inquiry ever widening.

The process by which a character assumes the significance of being peculiar, his antics weird, yet **harmless**, in such a community is often involute[97] and pathetic. This day, as has been said, saw Reifsneider at other doors, eagerly asking his unnatural question, and leaving a trail of amazement, sympathy, and pity in his wake. Although the authorities were informed – the county sheriff[98], no less[99] – it was not **deemed** advisable to take him into custody[100]; for when those who knew old Henry, and had for so long, reflected on the condition of the county insane asylum, a place which, because of the poverty of the district, was of **staggering** aberration[101] and sickening

94 *old fashioned:* going to a place
95 *formal:* to have something to eat or drink
96 *formal:* forcing
97 *unusual:* complicated
98 *US:* the most senior police officer in a county
99 used for emphasising that the person or thing you are talking about is very important
100 a situation in which someone is kept in prison until they go to court for trial
101 something that is not normal and not what you would normally expect

environment, it was decided to let him remain at large[102]; for, strange to relate[103], it was found on investigation that at night he returned peaceably enough to his lonesome[104] domicile[105] there to discover whether his wife had returned, and to brood in loneliness until the morning. Who would lock up a thin, eager, seeking old man with iron-gray hair and an attitude of kindly, innocent inquiry, particularly when he was well known for a past of only kindly servitude[106] and reliability? Those who had known him best rather agreed that he would be allowed to **roam** at large. He could do no harm. There were many who were willing to help him as to food, old clothes, the odds and ends[107] of his daily life – at least at first. His figure after a time became not so much a common-place[108] as an accepted curiosity, and the replies, "Why, no, Henry; I ain't seen her," or "No, Henry; she ain't been here today," more customary.

For several years thereafter[109] then he was an odd figure in the sun and rain, on dusty roads and muddy ones, encountered occasionally in strange and unexpected places, pursuing his endless search. Under-nourishment, after a time, although the neighbors and those who knew his history gladly contributed from their store, affected his body; for he walked much and ate little. The longer he roamed the public highway in this manner, the deeper became his strange hallucination; and finding it harder and harder to return from his more and more distant pilgrimages[110], he finally began taking a few utensils[111] with him from his home, making a small package of them, in order that

---

102 *phrase 'at large'*: free to walk around, not caught
103 *formal*: to tell someone about something that has happened or what someone has said
104 isolated or alone
105 *formal*: home
106 *formal*: the position of someone who is a slave or someone who is completely controlled by another person
107 scraps, small leftover pieces that are not valuable or important
108 something that is not unusual
109 *formal*: after a particular time that has been mentioned
110 a trip that a religious person makes to a holy place
111 something that you use to cook or eat with

he might not be compelled[112] to return. In an old **tin** coffee-pot of large size he placed a small tin cup, a knife, fork, and spoon, some salt and pepper, and to the outside of it, by a string forced through a **pierced** hole, he fastened a plate, which could be released, and which was his woodland table. It was no trouble for him to secure the little food that he needed, and with a strange, almost religious dignity, he had no hesitation in asking for that much. By degrees his hair became longer and longer, his once black hat became an earthen[113] brown, and his clothes threadbare[114] and dusty.

For all of three years he walked, and none knew how wide were his perambulations[115], nor how he survived the storms and cold. They could not see him, with **homely** rural understanding and forethought[116], sheltering[117] himself in hay-cocks, or by the sides of cattle, whose warm bodies protected him from the cold, and whose dull understandings were not opposed to his harmless presence. Overhanging rocks and trees kept him at times from the rain, and a friendly hay-loft[118] or corn-crib[119] was not above his **humble** consideration.

The involute progression of hallucination is strange. From asking at doors and being constantly rebuffed[120] or denied, he finally came to the conclusion that although his Phœbe might not be in any of the houses at the doors of which he inquired, she might nevertheless be within the sound of his voice. And so, from patient inquiry, he began to call sad, occasional cries, that ever and anon[121] waked the quiet landscapes and hill regions,

112 forced, obliged
113 made of dirt or clay
114 very thin and almost with holes in them because the material has been worn or used a lot
115 *formal, old fashioned*: to walk around a place slowly or for pleasure
116 careful thought and planning that prepares you well for a future event
117 to protect from bad weather
118 area at the top of a farm building used for storing hay
119 a large box for storing corn
120 *formal*: rejected bluntly
121 *phrase 'ever and anon'*: again and again

and set to echoing his thin "O-o-o Phœbe! O-o-o Phœbe!" It had a pathetic, albeit[122] insane, ring[123], and many a farmer or plowboy[124] came to know it even from afar and say, "There goes old Reifsneider."

Another thing that puzzled him greatly after a time and after many hundreds of inquiries was, when he no longer had any particular door-yard in view and no special inquiry to make, which way to go. These cross-roads, which occasionally led in four or even six directions, came after a time to puzzle him. But to solve this knotty[125] problem, which became more and more of a puzzle, there came to his aid another hallucination. Phœbe's spirit or some power of the air or wind or nature would tell him. If he stood at the centre of the parting of the ways, closed his eyes, turned thrice about[126] and called "O-o-o Phœbe!" twice, and then threw his cane straight before him, that would surely indicate which way to go for Phœbe, or one of these mystic powers would surely govern its direction and fall! In whichever direction it went, even though, as was not infrequently the case, it took him back along the path he had already come, or across fields, he was not so far gone in his mind but that he gave himself **ample** time to search before he called again. Also the hallucination seemed to persist that at some time he would surely find her. There were hours when his feet were sore, and his limbs weary, when he would stop in the heat to wipe his seamed brow, or in the cold to beat his arms. Sometimes, after throwing away his cane, and finding it indicating the direction from which he had just come, he would shake his head wearily and philosophically, as if contemplating the unbelievable or an untoward[127] **fate**, and then start briskly off. His strange figure came finally to be known in the farthest reaches[128] of three or

---

122 *formal*: used for introducing a comment that slightly changes or reduces the effect of what you said before it
123 a particular quality that something seems to have
124 farmer's assistant
125 difficult to solve or understand
126 *old-fashioned*: three times around
127 not appropriate, usual or normal
128 *phrase 'farthest reaches'*: the most distant or mysterious parts of something

four counties. Old Reifsneider was a pathetic character. His fame was wide.

Near a little town called Watersville, in Green County, perhaps four miles from that minor center of human activity, there was a place or **precipice** locally known as the Red Cliff, a sheer wall of red sandstone[130], perhaps a hundred feet high, which raised its sharp face for half a mile or more above the fruitful corn-fields and orchards that lay beneath, and which was surmounted[131] by a thick grove of trees. The slope that slowly led up to it from the opposite side was covered by a rank[132] growth of beech, hickory, and ash[133], through which threaded[134] a number of wagon-tracks[135] crossing at various angles. In fair weather it had become old Reifsneider's habit, so inured[136] was he by now to the open, to make his bed in some such[137] patch of trees as this to fry his bacon or boil his eggs at the foot of some tree before laying himself down for the night. Occasionally, so light and inconsequential was his sleep, he would walk at night. More often, the moonlight or some sudden wind stirring in the trees or a reconnoitring[138] animal arousing him, he would sit up and think, or pursue his quest[139] in the moonlight or the dark, a strange, unnatural, half wild, half savage-looking but utterly harmless creature, calling at lonely road crossings, staring at dark and shuttered houses, and wondering where, where Phœbe could really be.

That particular lull[139] that comes in the systole-diastole[140] of

129 a type of stone, used for building, made from sand that has become hard over many years
130 to surmount something is to be on top of it
131 *mainly literary*: growing and spreading too much
132 *beech, hickory* and *ash* – types of trees
133 to thread is to put something long and thin through a hole or space
134 the marks made by a wagon, a four-wheel vehicle usually pulled by horses and used for carrying heavy loads
135 *formal*: so familiar with an unpleasant experience that you no longer become upset by it
136 phrase 'some such': like this or similar to this one
137 getting information about an area (especially military information)
138 *mainly literary*: a long, difficult search
139 a quiet period during a very active or violent situation
140 *medical*: usually refers to the movement of the heart, the contraction and dilation; the earth is compared to a living thing that seems to stop breathing for a moment

this earthly ball at two o'clock in the morning invariably aroused him, and though he might not go any farther he would sit up and contemplate the darkness or the stars, wondering. Sometimes in the strange processes of his mind he would fancy[141] that he saw moving among the trees the figure of his lost wife, and then he would get up to follow, taking his utensils, always on a string, and his cane. If she seemed to **evade** him too easily he would run, or plead[142] or, suddenly losing track[143] of the fancied figure, stand awed[144] or disappointed, grieving for the moment over the almost insurmountable[145] difficulties of his search.

It was in the seventh year of these hopeless peregrinations[146], in the dawn of a similar springtime to that in which his wife had died, that he came at last one night to the vicinity of this self-same[147] patch that crowned[148] the rise to the Red Cliff. His far-flung[149] cane, used as a divining-rod[150] at the last cross-roads, had brought him hither[151]. He had walked many, many miles. It was after ten o'clock at night, and he was very weary. Long wandering and little eating had left him but a shadow of his former self[152]. It was a question now not so much of physical strength but of spiritual endurance which kept him up. He had scarcely eaten this day, and now exhausted he set himself down in the dark to rest and possibly to sleep.

Curiously on this occasion a strange suggestion of the presence of his wife surrounded him. It would not be long now, he counselled[153] with himself, although the long months had

141 *literary*: to believe or imagine that something is true
142 ask for something in an urgent or emotional way
143 *phrase 'losing track'*: not knowing any more where someone or something is or what is happening
144 feeling great respect, admiration, or sometimes fear for something
145 *formal*: impossible to deal with successfully
146 *formal*: a long trip
147 *formal*: used for emphasizing that something is exactly the same as another thing
148 *literary*: to cover the top of something
149 *mainly literary*: usually very distant, here, thrown over long distances
150 a Y-shaped stick used to search for underground water
151 *old-fashioned*: here
152 *phrase 'shadow of former self'*: much less healthy or successful or in much worse condition than before
153 talked to himself, gave himself advice

brought him nothing, until he should see her, talk to her. He fell asleep after a time, his head on his knees. At midnight the moon began to rise, and at two in the morning, his wakeful[155] hour, was a large silver disk shining through the trees to the east. He opened his eyes when the radiance became strong, making a silver pattern at his feet and lighting the woods with strange lusters[156] and silvery, shadowy forms. As usual, his old notion that his wife must be near occurred to him on this occasion, and he looked about him with a **speculative**, anticipatory eye. What was it that moved in the distant shadows along the path by which he had entered – a pale, flickering will-o'-the-wisp[157] that bobbed gracefully among the trees and riveted[158] his expectant gaze? Moonlight and shadows combined to give it a strange form and a stranger reality, this fluttering of bog-fire[159] or dancing of wandering fire-flies[160]. Was it truly his lost Phœbe? By a circuitous[161] route it passed about him, and in his fevered[162] state he fancied that he could see the very eyes of her, not as she was when he last saw her in the black dress and shawl but now a strangely younger Phœbe, gayer[163], sweeter, the one whom he had known years before as a girl. Old Reifsneider got up. He had been expecting and dreaming of this hour all these years, and now as he saw the feeble light dancing lightly before him he **peered** at it questioningly, one thin hand in his gray hair.

Of a sudden[164] there came to him now for the first time in many years the full charm of her girlish figure as he had known it in boyhood, the pleasing, sympathetic smile, the brown hair, the blue sash[165] she had once worn about her waist at a picnic,

154 not able to sleep
155 *mainly literary*: reflected light
156 a light that you sometimes see at night, floating above the ground, and caused by the combustion of natural gases; also, a person or thing that is difficult or impossible to catch or reach
157 to interest someone so much that they pay complete attention
158 a light that appears sometimes on marshland, caused by the combustion of natural gases
159 nocturnal beetles with organs at the back of their abdomen that produce light
160 longer than it needs to be because it is not direct
161 extremely excited or nervous
162 *old-fashioned*: happier, more excited
163 (more usual: *all of a sudden*) suddenly
164 a long, wide piece of cloth that you wrap around your waist like a belt

her gay, graceful movements. He walked around the base of the tree, straining with his eyes, forgetting for once his cane and utensils, and following eagerly after. On she moved before him, a will-o'-the-wisp of the spring, a little flame above her head, and it seemed as though among the small saplings[165] of ash and beech and the thick trunks of hickory and elm that she signalled with a young, a lightsome[166] hand.

"O Phœbe! Phœbe!" he called. "Have yuh really come? Have yuh really answered me?" And hurrying faster, he fell once, **scrambling** lamely[167] to his feet, only to see the light in the distance dancing illusively[168] on. On and on he hurried until he was fairly running, brushing his **ragged** arms against the trees, striking his hands and face against impeding[169] twigs[170]. His hat was gone, his lungs were breathless, his reason quite astray[171], when coming to the edge of the cliff he saw her below among a silvery bed of apple-trees now **blooming** in the spring.

"O Phœbe!" he called. "O Phœbe! Oh, no don't leave me!" And feeling the lure[172] of a world where love was young and Phœbe as this vision presented her, a delightful epitome[173] of their quondam[174] youth, he gave a gay cry of "Oh, wait, Phœbe!" and **leaped**.

Some farmer-boys, reconnoitring this region of bounty[175] and prospect[176] some few days afterward, found first the tin utensils tied together under the tree where he had left them, and then later at the foot of the cliff, pale, broken, but **elated**, a molded[177] smile of peace and delight upon his lips, his body. His old hat

165 young trees
166 *literary*: light, graceful or elegant in appearance
167 the way a person moves when their foot or leg is damaged and prevents them from walking easily
168 *formal*: not real but with an appearance of being real
169 blocking the way
170 small tree branches
171 lost, out of place
172 attraction to something which promises pleasure or gain
173 the best possible example of a particular type of person or thing
174 *literary*: previous, former
175 *literary*: good things in large amounts
176 potential for the future, especially something good
177 given a particular shape or form

was discovered lying under some low-growing saplings the twigs of which had held it back. No one of all the simple population knew how eagerly and joyously he had found his lost mate.

Post-reading exercises

Understanding the story

1 **Use these questions to help you check that you have understood the story.**

Henry and Phœbe

1 Where is the story set, in the town or the country?
2 What kind of house do Henry and Phœbe live in? Who owned part of the house before them? Who built the newer part of the house?
3 What is the furniture in the house like?
4 How long has Henry lived in the house? And Phœbe?
5 How many children does Henry have now? Where are they?
6 How do Henry and Phœbe live? What are their main occupations?
7 How old is Henry when Phœbe dies?
8 Why does Henry sometimes get cross with Phœbe?
9 What does Phœbe sometimes threaten to do? Does Henry believe her?
10 How old is Phœbe when she dies?

Henry

11 How does Henry feel about living alone?
12 Why doesn't Henry go and live with his children after Phœbe dies?
13 What happens to the house after Phœbe dies?
14 What does Henry see five months after his wife's death? What effect does this have on him?
15 What does Henry tell himself about Phœbe? What does he decide to do?

Henry's search

16 What does Henry ask Farmer Dodge? How does Dodge react?
17 What does Henry ask Mrs Race? How does she react?
18 Where does Henry go after he leaves Mrs Race?
19 Why isn't Henry sent to the insane asylum?
20 How long does Henry walk around the countryside looking for Phœbe?
21 What does Henry take with him on his trips? Why?
22 How does Henry decide in which direction to look for Phœbe?
23 How long has Henry been looking for Phœbe when he arrives at the Red Cliff?
24 What does he see when he wakes up during the night?
25 What happens when Henry starts running?
26 What do the farmer-boys find a few days later?

Language study

Vocabulary

The use of simile and metaphor

A simile is a figure of speech comparing one thing with another thing of a different kind to show similarity e.g. *The trees looked like long black fingers*. A metaphor is when a word or phrase with one meaning is applied directly to something different to suggest similarity e.g *He was an elephant of a man*.

1 Look at these extracts from the story. What similes and metaphors can you find?

   The creaky wooden loom ... stood like a dusty, bony skeleton [page 41].

   You perhaps know how it is with simple natures that fasten themselves like lichens on the stones of circumstance and weather their days to a crumbling conclusion [page 42].

   All the rest of life is a far-off, clamorous phantasmagoria, flickering like Northern lights in the night, and sounding as faintly as cow-bells tinkling in the distance [page 43].

   Phœbe Ann was thin and shapeless, a very umbrella of a woman, clad in shabby black [page 43].

   It was one of those little wisps of mist ... that ... flicker like small white cypresses of fog before they disappear [page 48].

   The ... moon was a large silver disk shining through the trees [page 59].

2 What is being described in each case? Which similes and metaphors do you find most effective?

Compound adjectives

These are adjectives made up of two or more words. They are a characteristic feature of Dreiser's writing. Some of them are quite common, e.g:

old-fashioned
half-open
run-down
broken-down
time-worn

Others are 'invented' or more poetic e.g.:

lead-and-pink-colored [page 41]
long-pendulumed [page 44]
tax-eaten [page 44]
green-lichen-covered [page 46]

3 Which object does *long-pendulumed* describe?

4 What colour do you think *lead* is?

5 What does *tax-eaten* refer to?

6 What is another way of saying *green-lichen-covered*?

The ending *-ed* is can be used to turn nouns into adjectives. The meaning of *-ed* in these cases is similar to *with* or *having* e.g. lime-stained = stained with lime.

7 How can these adjectives be expressed as phrases?

a) long-pendulumed
b) double-weighted
c) high-backed

When a noun is used as an adjective before another noun, it is usually singular even if the meaning is plural e.g. worm-eaten = eaten by worms.

8 Rewrite these sentences using a compound adjective.

1 The garden was covered in leaves.
   The garden was leaf-covered.
2 He sat down on the sofa with a low back.
3 The old cups were stained with tea.
4 The baby's ears were like shells.
5 The old man's face was beaten by the weather.
6 Henry was someone that everyone in the area knew well.

Grammar

Multiple-clause sentences

Dreiser often uses longer, multiple-clause sentences, especially when he is describing buildings or surroundings.

Look at this extract describing the newer part of the house which Henry added to the older part built by his grandfather.

> *The new portion, of now rain-beaten, time-worn slabs, through which the wind squeaked in chinks at times, and which several overshadowing elms and a butternut-tree made picturesque and reminiscently pathetic, but a little damp, was erected by Henry when he was twenty-one and just married* [page 40].

Notice how all this information can be broken down into separate sentences:

> The new portion of now rain-beaten, time-worn slabs, was erected by Henry.
> He was twenty-one. He was just married.
> The wind squeaked through the chinks at times.
> Several overshadowing elms and a butternut-tree made it picturesque and reminiscently pathetic.
> They also made it damp.

Notice how Dreiser uses *through which* and *which* to connect the clauses describing the house.

Here is another example. This extract describes the carpet made by Phœbe.

> *The rag carpet that underlay all these sturdy examples of enduring furniture was a weak, faded, lead-and-pink-colored affair woven by Phœbe Ann's own hands, when she was fifteen years younger than she was when she died* [page 41].

9 Try and break down the above sentence into shorter sentences. Use these phrases to help you.

> The rag carpet was …
> It underlay …
> It had been woven …
> She was then fifteen …

10 Do the same with this sentence.

His hat was gone, his lungs were breathless, his reason quite astray, when coming to the edge of the cliff he saw her below among a silvery bed of apple-trees now blooming in the spring [page 60].

The use of preposition + *which*

Dreiser often uses a preposition followed by *which* to introduce a new clause. This is quite a formal structure. Look at this example:

*His old hat was discovered lying under some low-growing saplings the twigs **of which** held it back* [page 60].

This could be expressed using two separate sentences:

His old hat was discovered lying under some low-growing saplings. The twigs of the saplings held the hat back.

In more modern English, the pronoun *whose* could also be used:

*His old hat was discovered lying under some low-growing saplings **whose** twigs held it back.*

11 Look at these examples from the story and underline the preposition + *which*. How could you express the same ideas without using preposition + *which*?

Example:

The chickens, of which formerly there was a large flock, had almost disappeared.

The chickens had almost disappeared. Formerly, there was a large flock of them.

The moon shone through the east windows, throwing the pattern of the panes on the wooden floor, and making the old furniture, to which he was accustomed, stand out dimly in the room.

The slope that slowly led up to it from the opposite side was covered by a rank growth of beech, hickory, and ash, through which threaded a number of wagon-tracks crossing at various angles.

12 Write the following as single sentences using a preposition + *which*.

1 We rode under a bridge. It was from the 18th century.
2 I sent a letter to this address. It's the wrong one.
3 We travelled through different countries. They were very interesting.
4 The plane flew over enemy territory. It was full of danger.
5 I belong to an environmental group. It is very influential.

6 We stopped at an old farmhouse. It had a *Vacancies* sign in the window.

Literary analysis
Plot
1 Look at these events from the story and number them in the correct order.
   a) Henry meets Farmer Dodge on the road.
   b) Some boys find Henry's body.
   c) Henry packs some utensils so that he doesn't need to return to the farm every night.
   d) Phœbe falls ill and dies.
   e) Henry goes to see Matilda Race.
   f) Henry's parents die.
   g) Henry's grandfather builds a house made of logs.
   h) Henry sees Phœbe among the trees from the top of the cliff.
   i) Henry dreams that Phœbe comes to him and touches his shoulder.
   j) Henry and Phœbe get married.
2 Is the plot simple or complicated? Does the story end as you expected?

Character
3 Look at these pairs of words describing Henry. Choose the more suitable word in each case and justify your choice.
   independent/dependent
   honest/dishonest
   loving/cold
   hard-working/lazy
   proud/greedy
   religious/sceptical
   Think of three more adjectives to describe Henry.
4 Why do you think Henry goes mad? Do you think it could have been avoided? Why/why not?
5 What kind of person is Phœbe? How would you describe her relationship with her husband?
6 What impression do you have of the other characters in the story? Think about Farmer Dodge and Mrs Race. What do they tell us about the kind of community in which Henry lives?

Narration

7 Dreiser tells us a lot about Henry's house, furniture and surroundings. Why do you think he does this?
8 How does Dreiser use direct speech to reveal character? What do we learn about Henry and Phœbe from their conversations? What do we learn about the neighbours?
9 Do you think Dreiser 'moralises' in the story? Is he trying to teach us something about human nature?
10 What is Dreiser's attitude to his characters? Does he look down on them or is he sympathetic?
11 Is the story critical of society in any way? What might have happened to Henry in the USA/your own country today?

Atmosphere

12 How does Dreiser convey the isolation of Henry and Phœbe's lives?
13 Is there a difference between the atmosphere of the story before and after Phœbe's death?
14 Is there humour in the story? Where?
15 What is the overall atmosphere of the story? How does it make you feel?
16 Is it fair to describe *The Lost Phœbe* as a ghost story?
17 Is the end of the story happy? Why/why not?

Style

18 Dreiser writes in long, sometimes formal sentences, and he uses a wide variety of vocabulary. In which parts of the story is this particularly true?
19 What effect does the dialogue of the characters have? Is there a good balance between dialogue and description?
20 Sometimes, Dreiser addresses the reader directly, e.g. *You have seen the what-not of cherry wood, perhaps* …; *You perhaps know how it is with simple natures* … . What effect does this have?

Guidance to the above literary terms, answer keys to all the exercises and activities, plus a wealth of other reading-practice material, can be found on the student's section of the Macmillan Readers website at: www.macmillanenglish.com/readers.

The Baby Party
by F Scott Fitzgerald

About the author

Francis Scott Key Fitzgerald was born in 1896 in St Paul, Minnesota in the USA. He is best known for his novels about life in the US 'Jazz Age' which took place during the 1920s.

Fitzgerald was encouraged to write by his teachers at school and he wrote stories for the school magazine. Even at Princeton University, his writing was more important to him than his studies. He joined the army in 1917 and the following summer, when he was at an army camp in Alabama, he met and fell in love with Zelda Sayre. She was the young and beautiful 18-year-old daughter of a rich family. He desperately wanted to marry her, but Zelda wanted someone who was wealthy and successful.

Determined to win her, Fitzgerald worked hard on his first novel, *This Side of Paradise*. It was published in 1920, sold well, and made Fitzgerald rich. Zelda and he were married, and moved to New York, where he wrote a second novel, *The Beautiful and Damned*. This was also a success, and the Fitzgeralds began to live a life of luxury and excess. Their daughter Frances was born in 1921.

Both Fitzgerald and Zelda suffered from health problems, which were made worse by their heavy drinking. In 1925, when they were living in France, *The Great Gatsby* was published, but it did not enjoy the same commercial success as his other novels. The Fitzgeralds moved back to the USA where, in 1930, Zelda had a nervous breakdown. Her treatment was expensive: when *Tender is the Night* was published in 1934, Fitzgerald hoped it would pay their debts. But it was not a great success, and by now Scott himself was ill.

In 1937, Fitzgerald moved to Hollywood to work as a screenwriter while Zelda stayed behind. He fell in love with Sheilah Graham, a journalist, and spent the rest of his life with her. Fitzgerald's last novel was *The Last Tycoon*, which remained unfinished when he died of a heart attack in 1940. Zelda died in 1948, in a fire at the clinic where she was being treated.

Ironically, the novels which were less successful in Fitzgerald's lifetime are now thought to be his best. Several of his books have been made into films, including *The Great Gatsby* and *Tender is the Night*. In addition to his novels, Fitzgerald also wrote over 150 short stories.

About the story

The Baby Party was first published in *Hearst's International* in 1925. It was later published in the collection *All the Sad Young Men*.

Background information

Children in the 1920s

Fitzgerald writes particularly well about a father's love for his little girl and the pride of parents in their children. He himself had a daughter, Frances, and is no doubt drawing on first-hand experience in his description of the child and her actions. He may also have attended a 'baby party' similar to the one in the story. The competitive attitude of the mothers and the behaviour of the children is described with humour and affection.

Fitzgerald writes that the children were *modern babies* and that they behaved well. He notes that they *ate and slept at regular hours, so their dispositions were good* and adds that *such a party would not have been possible thirty years ago*. The story takes place at a time when bringing up children was a full-time job for most mothers who did not work outside the home.

Middle class, suburban America

John and Edith Andros's style of life is that of a relatively prosperous couple who live in the suburbs and can afford a maid. We are told they have *endless servant problems*. John travels by train every day to his office in the city; Edith seems to be a full-time housewife. Next door, the Markeys' life seems to follow a similar pattern.

Appearances are very important to the families in the story. It is important that the children are dressed well and behave well at the party. There is competition among the mothers to see whose child is the best. Social status is important: Edith thinks that Mrs Markey is *common* and not as good as her. When the women argue and John and Joe fight to defend their families' honour, Fitzgerald shows us the passions and suppressed violence underneath the calm surface of suburbia.

Summary

It may help you to know something about what happens in the story before you read it. Don't worry, this summary does *not* tell you how the story ends!

John Andros is 38 and lives in a suburban town with his wife Edith and two-year-old-daughter Ede. Every day, he commutes by train to work in an office in the city.

The story takes place on the day of a baby party at the house of the Markeys. The Markeys live next door to John and Edith and have a little boy, Billy. Edith and Mrs Markey do not like each other but John and Joe Markey travel to work together and are quite friendly.

There are 13 babies at the party, all with their mothers. Time passes and the children grow noisier and livelier. They have something to eat and, soon afterwards, people begin to leave. Several fathers arrive to take their children home. Edith is anxious because John has not yet arrived and it is six o'clock. She wants him to see little Ede with the other children.

Ede suddenly sees Billy Markey across the room. He is holding a teddy bear and she decides she wants it. She pulls the bear from his arms. Billy tries to get it back and Ede pushes him to the floor. Billy's parents try to intervene but Ede again pushes Billy backwards. This time, the little boy hits his head on the floor and begins to cry. Ede laughs. Before she can stop herself, Edith laughs too. Mrs Markey is furious. Ede, seeing the effect she has produced, laughs again and soon her mother is also laughing helplessly. Mrs Markey tells Edith to leave the house and take her *brat* with her. Edith begins to cry and insults the Markeys. Mrs Markey orders her husband to send Edith out of the house. At this moment, John arrives and finds his wife in tears. Joe Markey tells him that his family is responsible for all the trouble.

Edith leaves with her child and Joe Markey challenges John to a fight. They fight together silently and furiously in the snow until both of them are bleeding and their clothes are torn. They finally stop fighting when they hear someone coming towards them. They shake hands and say goodnight.

Later that night, when John and Edith are looking at Ede asleep in her bed, the maid announces that the Markeys are at the door.

Pre-reading exercises

Key vocabulary

This section will help you familiarise yourself with some of the more specific vocabulary used in the story. You may want to use it to help you before you start reading, or as a revision exercise after you have finished the story.

Verbs to describe action or movement

The party

1 **Look at the words and phrases in the left-hand column below and match them with the correct definitions in the right-hand column.**

1	**grab**	a)	to hit someone or something so that they fall down
2	**finger**	b)	to take hold of something in a rough or rude way
3	**round**	c)	to take something quickly in your hand
4	**break away / break loose**	d)	to touch or feel something with your fingers
5	**rush**	e)	to accidentally hit part of your body against something, making it hurt
6	**squirm**	f)	to pull someone or something by making a short, strong movement
7	**knock over**	g)	to escape from a person, place or situation
8	**bump**	h)	to hurry in order to get somewhere very quickly
9	**seize**	i)	to move around something
10	**tug**	j)	to move by twisting and turning in a small space

2 **Complete this paragraph using a suitable form of the verbs above. More than one answer may be correct in some cases.**

At first the child sat shyly on her mother's knee, *fingering* the edge of her dress. Then she began to .... around because she wanted to be down. Suddenly she .... from her mother and .... towards the little boy. She .... him over and .... the toy from his hands. The boy had .... his head on the floor and he began to cry. Furious, he jumped up and .... the table in order to reach the girl. He .... hold

72 | *The Baby Party*

of her hair and .... it hard. She eventually .... and ran back to her mother.

The fight

3 Look at the words and phrases in the left-hand column below and match them with the correct definitions in the right-hand column.

1	**toss**	a)	to try hard to do something
2	**slip**	b)	to walk in an uncontrolled way as if you are going to fall over
3	**swing**	c)	to change the position of your body when you are lying down
4	**thresh about**	d)	if you do this, your feet slide accidentally and you lose your balance or fall over
5	**strain**	e)	to throw something in a careless way
6	**roll**	f)	to walk with difficulty because of an injured leg or foot
7	**stagger**	g)	to try to hit someone by making a smooth, curving movement with your arm
8	**limp**	h)	to move your body in a violent, uncontrolled way

4 Choose the best verb to complete these sentences.

1 The old man slipped/strained on the ice and broke his hip.
2 Sue limped/tossed the ball to another player and walked off the field.
3 The spy jumped from the moving train and staggered/rolled over several times.
4 After he was hit on the head, Jack felt dizzy and strained/staggered to the nearest chair.
5 The dog is limping/swinging; he must have hurt his paw.
6 The boxer swung/strained to sit up but he was too weak.
7 I knew he was in pain when I saw him rolling/slipping around on the floor.
8 The boys threshed/strained about and tossed/swung their arms in an effort to hit each other.

The Baby Party

Words to describe noise

5 **Look at the words and phrases in the left-hand column below and match them with the correct definitions in the right-hand column.**

1 **drown out**   a) to say something in a loud voice or make a loud noise because you are angry, afraid, excited or in pain
2 **wail**   b) to talk in a quiet voice that is difficult to hear especially because you are annoyed or embarrassed or are talking to yourself
3 **yell**   c) to shout or cry with a long, high sound to show that you are in pain or very sad
4 **mutter**   d) to prevent a sound from being heard by making a louder noise
5 **burst out**   e) a sudden noisy breath that is usually caused by surprise, shock or pain
6 **gasp (n)**   f) to suddenly say or shout something

6 **Complete these sentences using a suitable form of the above words.**

1 I don't like teachers who .... at the children all the time.
2 The shouts of the children .... all other noise.
3 Sam spoke in a low voice to his wife: 'I've got to get out of here,' he ....
4 When the boy pulled her hair, little Gina .... and ran to her mother.
5 Mrs Brown gave a .... of horror when she saw the mess the children had made.
6 She tried to control her temper but it was impossible. 'Go home right now!' she suddenly ....

Main themes

Before you read the story, you may want to think about some of its main themes. The questions will help you think about the story as you are reading it for the first time. There is more discussion of the main themes in the *Literary analysis* section after the story.

Love

Fitzgerald looks at several different forms of love and friendship: the love between husband and wife (John and Ede, the Markeys), love between friends (John and Joe), and the love of parents for their children. Parental love is perhaps given the most emphasis: Fitzgerald describes very vividly the fierce love and protection that mothers and fathers feel for their children. John fights with Joe to defend his wife and child, but it is the thought that little Ede has been insulted that really pushes him into physical violence with a man who is his friend. He recognises this at the end of the story as he holds his sleeping child and acknowledges what he has fought for *so savagely*.

7 As you read the story, ask yourself:

a) Are the different relationships described realistically?
b) Which relationships are important to John?

Frustration

We know that John's life has not been easy up to now. We are told that he has had to fight poverty, and ill health and although he is only thirty-eight, he does not hold many illusions about life. His life is one of routine – travelling to and from an office in the city. We are not told in which ways John has found life disappointing, but a sense of frustration seems to cling to him. When he fights with Joe, he seems to be expressing a lot of repressed violence and resentment. The fight is about more than what happens at the party and gives John a kind of relief from his frustrations.

Fitzgerald himself felt frustration as a young man: his books did not always do as well as he hoped, and he and his wife experienced ill health and money problems. One feels that John and his inner feelings are based, at least partly, on the author's experiences and struggles.

8 As you read the story, ask yourself:

a) What indications are there that John is frustrated with his life?
b) Which aspects of Fitzgerald's own life are reflected in the story?

★ ★ ★ ★

The Baby Party

by F Scott Fitzgerald

When John Andros felt old he found solace¹ in the thought of life continuing through his child. The dark trumpets of oblivion were less loud at the **patter** of his child's feet or at the sound of his child's voice babbling mad non sequiturs² to him over the telephone. The latter incident occurred every afternoon at three when his wife called the office from the country, and he came to look forward to it as one of the vivid minutes of his day.

He was not physically old, but his life had been a series of struggles up a series of rugged hills, and here at thirty-eight having won his battles against ill-health and poverty he cherished³ less than the usual number of illusions. Even his feeling about his little girl was qualified. She had interrupted his rather intense love-affair with his wife, and she was the reason for their living in a suburban town, where they paid for country air with endless servant troubles and the weary merry-go-round⁴ of the commuting⁵ train.

It was little Ede as a definite piece of youth that chiefly interested him. He liked to take her on his lap⁶ and examine minutely her fragrant, downy⁷ scalp and her eyes with their irises of morning blue. Having paid this homage John was content that the nurse should take her away. After ten minutes the very vitality of the child irritated him; he was inclined to lose his temper when things were broken, and one Sunday afternoon when she had **disrupted** a bridge game⁸ by permanently hiding

1 something that makes you feel better when you are sad or upset
2 a statement that does not have a connection with what was said before
3 believed something is of value because it is important to you
4 a continuous series of related events or activities
5 travelling regularly to and from work
6 the top part of the legs when sitting down
7 covered in soft small hairs
8 a card game for four players who make two teams

up the ace of spades[9], he had made a scene that had reduced his wife to tears.

This was absurd and John was ashamed of himself. It was inevitable that such things would happen, and it was impossible that little Ede should spend all her indoor hours in the nursery upstairs when she was becoming, as her mother said, more nearly a 'real person' every day.

She was two and a half, and this afternoon, for instance, she was going to a baby party. Grown-up Edith, her mother, had telephoned the information to the office, and little Ede had confirmed the business by shouting 'I yam going to a *pantry*!' into John's unsuspecting left ear.

'Drop in at the Markeys' when you get home, won't you, dear?' resumed her mother. 'It'll be funny. Ede's going to be all dressed up in her new pink dress – '

The conversation terminated abruptly with a squawk[10] which indicated that the telephone had been pulled violently to the floor. John laughed and decided to get an early train out; the **prospect** of a baby party in someone else's house amused him.

'What a peach of a mess[11]!' he thought humorously. 'A dozen mothers, and each one looking at nothing but her own child. All the babies breaking things and grabbing at the cake, and each mama going home thinking about the subtle superiority of her own child to every other child there.'

He was in a good humour today – all the things in his life were going better than they had ever gone before. When he got off the train at his station he shook his head at an importunate[12] taxi man, and began to walk up the long hill towards his house through the crisp December twilight[13]. It was only six o'clock but the moon was out, shining with proud brilliance on the thin sugary snow that lay over the lawns.

---

9 a card with one symbol like a pointed, black leaf; in a card game, it has either the highest or lowest value in a suit
10 a loud high noise like a bird
11 *informal, old-fashioned, phrase 'What a peach of a mess'*: a wonderful mess
12 *formal*: continuing to ask for something in a determined and annoying way
13 the light in the evening when the sky begins to get dark

As he walked along drawing his lungs full of cold air his happiness increased, and the idea of a baby party appealed to him more and more. He began to wonder how Ede compared to other children of her own age, and if the pink dress she was to wear was something radical and mature. Increasing his gait[14] he came in sight of his own house, where the lights of a **defunct** Christmas-tree still blossomed in the window, but he continued on past the walk[15]. The party was at the Markeys' next door.

As he mounted the brick step and rang the bell he became aware of voices inside, and he was glad he was not too late. Then he raised his head and listened – the voices were not children's voices, but they were loud and pitched high with anger; there were at least three of them and one, which rose as he listened to a hysterical sob[16], he recognised immediately as his wife's.

'There's been some trouble,' he thought quickly.

Trying the door, he found it unlocked and pushed it open.

The baby party started at half past four, but Edith Andros, calculating **shrewdly** that the new dress would stand out more sensationally against vestments[17] already rumpled[18], planned the arrival of herself and little Ede for five. When they appeared it was already a flourishing[19] affair. Four baby girls and nine baby boys, each one curled and washed and dressed with all the care of a proud and jealous heart, were dancing to the music of a phonograph[20]. Never more than two or three were dancing at once, but as all were continually in motion running to and from their mothers for encouragement, the general effect was the same.

As Edith and her daughter entered, the music was temporarily drowned out by a sustained chorus, consisting largely of the word *cute*[21] and directed towards little Ede, who stood looking timidly

14 the way that someone walks
15 *US:* a path across someone's grass or garden
16 the sound made when someone cries noisily
17 *formal:* clothes normally worn by a priest
18 untidy or not smooth
19 successful
20 *old-fashioned:* a record player
21 attractive, usually small, and easy to like

about and fingering the edges of her pink dress. She was not kissed – this is the sanitary age[22] – but she was passed along a row of mamas each one of whom said 'cu-u-ute' to her and held her pink little hand before passing her on to the next. After some encouragement and a few mild pushes she was absorbed into the dance, and became an active member of the party.

Edith stood near the door talking to Mrs Markey, and keeping an eye on the tiny figure in the pink dress. She did not care for Mrs Markey; she considered her both snippy[23] and common[24], but John and Joe Markey were congenial[25] and went in together on the commuting train every morning, so the two women kept up an elaborate **pretence** of warm amity[26]. They were always reproaching each other for 'not coming to see me', and they were always planning the kind of parties that began with 'You'll have to come to dinner with us soon, and we'll go to the theatre,' but never matured further.

'Little Ede looks perfectly darling[27],' said Mrs Markey, smiling and moistening her lips in a way that Edith found particularly repulsive. 'So *grown-up* – I can't *believe* it!'

Edith wondered if 'little Ede' referred to the fact that Billy Markey, though several months younger, weighed almost five pounds more. Accepting a cup of tea she took a seat with two other ladies on a divan and launched into the real business of the afternoon, which of course lay in relating the recent accomplishments and insouciances[28] of her child.

An hour passed. Dancing palled[29] and the babies took to sterner[30] sport. They ran into the dining-room, rounded the big table, and essayed[31] the kitchen door, from which they were rescued by an expeditionary force of mothers. Having been

22 phrase *'the sanitary age'*: relating to health, a time when people were aware of cleanliness
23 someone who is not patient and speaks to people in an angry way
24 an insulting way of describing someone from a low social class
25 friendly and enjoying the company of others
26 *formal*: a friendly relationship, especially between nations or groups of people
27 very attractive; people who use this word do not usually sound sincere
28 amusing or carefree activities
29 become less interesting
30 more serious
31 *military*: attempted

rounded up³² they immediately broke loose, and rushing back to the dining-room tried the familiar swinging door again. The word 'overheated' began to be used, and small white brows were dried with small white handkerchiefs. A general attempt to make the babies sit down began, but the babies squirmed off laps with peremptory³³ cries of 'Down! Down!' and the rush into the fascinating dining-room began anew.

This phase of the party came to an end with the arrival of refreshments, a large cake with two candles, and saucers of vanilla ice-cream. Billy Markey, a stout laughing baby with red hair and legs somewhat bowed³⁴, blew out the candles, and placed an experimental thumb on the white frosting³⁵. The refreshments were distributed, and the children ate, greedily but without confusion – they had behaved remarkably well all afternoon. They were modern babies who ate and slept at regular hours, so their dispositions³⁶ were good, and their faces healthy and pink – such a peaceful party would not have been possible thirty years ago.

After the refreshments a gradual exodus³⁷ began. Edith glanced anxiously at her watch – it was almost six, and John had not arrived. She wanted him to see Ede with the other children – to see how dignified and polite and intelligent she was, and how the only ice-cream spot on her dress was some that had dropped from her chin when she was joggled³⁸ from behind.

'You're a darling,' she whispered to her child, drawing³⁹ her suddenly against her knee. 'Do you know you're a darling? Do you *know* you're a darling?'

---

32 *phrase 'rounded up'*: brought together in a place for a particular purpose, especially cattle
33 *formal*: speaking or behaving rather rudely, as if you expect other people to obey you immediately
34 curved so that the knees do not meet
35 *US*: a smooth sweet substance usually made from sugar, butter and liquid, used for covering cakes
36 the way that someone normally thinks and behaves, that shows what type of person they are
37 when a lot of people leave a place or activity at the same time
38 *informal*: moved in different directions with sudden, quick movements
39 phrase '*drawing against*': moving someone towards you

Ede laughed. 'Bow-wow[40],' she said suddenly.

'Bow-wow?' Edith looked around. 'There isn't any bow-wow.'

'Bow-wow,' repeated Ede. 'I want a bow-wow.'

Edith followed the small pointing finger.

'That isn't a bow-wow, dearest, that's a teddy-bear[41].'

'Bear?'

'Yes, that's a teddy-bear, and it belongs to Billy Markey. You don't want Billy Markey's teddy-bear, do you?'

Ede did want it.

She broke away from her mother and approached Billy Markey, who held the toy closely in his arms. Ede stood regarding him with **inscrutable** eyes, and Billy laughed.

Grown-up Edith looked at her watch again, this time impatiently.

The party had dwindled[42] until, besides Ede and Billy, there were only two babies remaining – and one of the two remained only by virtue of[43] having hidden himself under the dining-room table. It was selfish of John not to come. It showed so little pride in the child. Other fathers had come, half a dozen of them, to call for their wives, and they had stayed for a while and looked on.

There was a sudden wail. Ede had obtained Billy's teddy-bear by pulling it forcibly from his arms, and on Billy's attempt to recover it, she had pushed him casually to the floor.

'Why, Ede!' cried her mother, repressing an inclination to laugh.

Joe Markey, a handsome, broad-shouldered man of thirty-five, picked up his son and set him on his feet. 'You're a fine fellow,' he said **jovially**. 'Let a girl knock you over! You're a fine fellow.'

'Did he bump his head?' Mrs Markey returned anxiously from bowing[44] the next to last remaining mother out of the door.

'No-o-o-o,' exclaimed Markey. 'He bumped something else, didn't you, Billy? He bumped something else.'

40 the noise a dog makes, used by children or when talking to children
41 a soft toy bear
42 become gradually less or smaller over a period of time until almost nothing remains
43 because of, or as a result of
44 *phrase 'bow out'*: saying goodbye

Billy had so far forgotten the bump that he was already making an attempt to recover his property. He seized a leg of the bear which projected from Ede's enveloping arms and tugged at it but without success.

'No,' said Ede emphatically.

Suddenly, encouraged by the success of her former half-accidental **manoeuvre**, Ede dropped the teddy-bear, placed her hands on Billy's shoulders and pushed him backward off his feet.

This time he landed less harmlessly; his head hit the bare floor just off the rug with a dull hollow sound, whereupon he drew in his breath[45] and delivered an agonized yell.

Immediately the room was in confusion. With an exclamation Markey hurried to his son, but his wife was first to reach the injured baby and catch him up into her arms.

'Oh, *Billy*,' she cried, 'what a terrible bump! She ought to be spanked[46].'

Edith, who had rushed immediately to her daughter, heard this remark, and her lips came sharply together.

'Why, Ede,' she whispered perfunctorily, 'you bad girl!'

Ede put back her little head suddenly and laughed. It was a loud laugh, a triumphant laugh with victory in it and challenge and **contempt**. Unfortunately it was also an infectious laugh. Before her mother realized the delicacy of the situation, she too had laughed, an audible, distinct laugh not unlike the baby's, and partaking of[47] the same overtones.

Then, as suddenly, she stopped.

Mrs Markey's face had grown red with anger, and Markey, who had been feeling the back of the baby's head with one finger, looked at her, **frowning**.

'It's **swollen** already,' he said with a note of reproof[48] in his voice. 'I'll get some witch-hazel[49].'

---

45 *phrase 'drew in his breath'*: take in a lot of air as you breathe
46 slapped or hit on the bottom with an open hand
47 *formal*: sharing
48 *formal*: criticism or blame
49 liquid used for rubbing on small cuts or injuries

But Mrs Markey had lost her temper. 'I don't see anything funny about a child being hurt!' she said in a **trembling** voice.

Little Ede meanwhile had been looking at her mother curiously. She noted that her own laugh had produced her mother's and she wondered if the same cause would always produce the same effect. So she chose this moment to throw back her head and laugh again.

To her mother the additional mirth[50] added the final touch of hysteria to the situation. Pressing her handkerchief to her mouth she **giggled** irrepressibly. It was more than nervousness – she felt that in a peculiar way she was laughing with her child – they were laughing together.

It was in a way a **defiance** – those two against the world.

While Markey rushed upstairs to the bathroom for ointment, his wife was walking up and down rocking the yelling boy in her arms.

'Please go home!' she broke out suddenly. 'The child's badly hurt, and if you haven't the decency to be quiet, you'd better go home.'

'Very well,' said Edith, her own temper rising. 'I've never seen anyone make such a mountain out of –'

'Get out!' cried Mrs Markey frantically. 'There's the door, get out – I never want to see you in our house again. You or your brat[51] either!'

Edith had taken her daughter's hand and was moving quickly towards the door, but at this remark she stopped and turned around, her face contracting with **indignation**.

'Don't you dare call her that!'

Mrs Markey did not answer but continued walking up and down, muttering to herself and to Billy in an inaudible voice.

Edith began to cry.

'I will get out!' she **sobbed**, 'I've never heard anybody so rude and c-common in my life. I'm glad your baby did get pushed down – he's nothing but a f-fat little fool anyhow.'

50 *mainly literary*: happy laughter
51 *informal*: an annoying child who behaves badly

The Baby Party

Joe Markey reached the foot of the stairs just in time to hear this remark.

'Why, Mrs Andros,' he said sharply, 'can't you see the child's hurt. You really ought to control yourself.'

'Control m-myself!' exclaimed Edith brokenly. 'You better ask her to c-control herself. I've never heard anybody so c-common in my life.'

'She's insulting me!' Mrs Markey was now livid with rage[52]. 'Did you hear what she said, Joe? I wish you'd put her out. If she won't go, just take her by the shoulders and put her out!'

'Don't you dare touch me!' cried Edith. 'I'm going just as quick as I can find my c-coat!'

Blind with tears she took a step toward the hall. It was just at this moment that the door opened and John Andros walked anxiously in.

'John!' cried Edith, and fled to him wildly.

'What's the matter? Why, what's the matter?'

'They're – they're putting me out!' she wailed, collapsing against him. 'He'd just started to take me by the shoulders and put me out. I want my coat!'

'That's not true,' objected Markey hurriedly. 'Nobody's going to put you out.' He turned to John. 'Nobody's going to put you out.' He turned to John. 'Nobody's going to put her out,' he repeated. 'She's –'

'What do you mean "put her out"?' demanded John **abruptly**. 'What's all this talk, anyhow?'

'Oh, let's go!' cried Edith. 'I want to go. They're so *common*, John!'

'Look here!' Markey's face darkened. 'You've said that about enough. You're acting sort of[53] crazy.'

'They called Ede a brat!'

———

For the second time that afternoon little Ede expressed emotion at an inopportune moment. Confused and frightened at the

---

52 *phrase 'livid with rage'*: extremely angry
53 *mainly spoken, phrase 'sort of'*: slightly or in some ways

shouting voices, she began to cry, and her tears had the effect of conveying[54] that she felt the insult in her heart.

'What's the idea of this?' broke out John. 'Do you insult your guests in your own house?'

'It seems to me it's your wife that's done the insulting!' answered Markey crisply. 'In fact, your baby there started all the trouble.'

John gave a contemptuous **snort**. 'Are you calling names at a little baby?' he inquired. 'That's a fine manly business!'

'Don't talk to him, John,' insisted Edith. 'Find my coat!'

'You must be in a bad way,' went on John angrily, 'if you have to take out your temper on[55] a helpless little baby.'

'I never heard anything so damn[56] twisted[57] in my life,' shouted Markey. 'If that wife of yours would shut her mouth for a minute –'

'Wait a minute! You're not talking to a woman and child now –'

There was an incidental interruption. Edith had been fumbling on a chair for her coat, and Mrs Markey had been watching her with hot, angry eyes. Suddenly she laid Billy down on the sofa, where he immediately stopped crying and pulled himself upright, and coming into the hall she quickly found Edith's coat and handed it to her without a word. Then she went back to the sofa, picked up Billy, and rocking him in her arms looked again at Edith with hot, angry eyes. The interruption had taken less than half a minute.

'Your wife comes in here and begins shouting around about how common we are,' burst out Markey violently. 'Well, if we're so damn common, you'd better stay away! And what's more, you'd better get out now!'

Again, John gave a short, contemptuous laugh.

---

54 communicating ideas or feelings indirectly
55 *phrase 'take out your temper on'*: make someone suffer because you are angry, upset or tired, even if it is not their fault
56 used for emphasising what you are saying, especially when you are angry about something
57 *informal*: behaving in a strange and cruel way

'You're not only common,' he returned, 'you're evidently an awful bully[58] – when there's any helpless women and children around.' He felt for the knob and swung the door open. 'Come on, Edith.'

Taking up her daughter in her arms, his wife stepped outside and John, still looking contemptuously at Markey, started to follow.

'Wait a minute!' Markey took a step forward; he was trembling slightly, and two large veins on his temples[59] were suddenly full of blood. 'You don't think you can get away with that, do you? With me?'

Without a word John walked out the door, leaving it open.

Edith, still weeping, had started for home. After following her with his eyes until she reached her own walk, John turned back towards the lighted doorway where Markey was slowly coming down the slippery steps. He took off his overcoat and hat, tossed them off the path onto the snow. Then, sliding a little on the iced walk, he took a step forward.

At the first **blow**, they both slipped and fell heavily to the sidewalk, half rising then, and again pulled each other on the ground. They found a better foothold in the thin snow to the side of the walk and rushed at each other, both swinging wildly and pressing out the snow into a pasty[60] mud underfoot.

The street was deserted, and except for their short tired gasps and the padded sound as one or the other slipped down into the slushy[61] mud, they fought in silence, clearly defined to each other by the full moonlight as well as by the amber glow that shone out of the open door. Several times they both slipped down together, and then for a while the conflict threshed about wildly on the lawn.

For ten, fifteen, twenty minutes they fought there senselessly in the moonlight. They had both taken off coats and vests at some silently agreed upon interval and now their shirts dripped

58 someone who frightens or hurts someone who is smaller and weaker than they are
59 the flat areas on either side of your forehead next to your eyes
60 like paste: a kind of glue often made with flour and water
61 used to describe snow that is starting to melt

from their backs in wet pulpy[62] shreds[63]. Both were torn and bleeding and so exhausted that they could stand only when by their position they mutually supported each other – the impact, the mere effort of a blow, would send them both to their hands and knees.

But it was not **weariness** that ended the business, and the very meaninglessness of the fight was a reason for not stopping. They stopped because once when they were straining at each other on the ground, they heard a man's footsteps coming along the sidewalk. They had rolled somehow into the shadow, and when they heard these footsteps they stopped fighting, stopped moving, stopped breathing, lay **huddled** together like two boys playing Indian[64] until the footsteps had passed. Then, staggering to their feet, they looked at each other like two drunken men.

'I'll be damned if I'm going on with this thing any more,' cried Markey thickly.

'I'm not going on any more either,' said John Andros. 'I've had enough of this thing.'

Again they looked at each other, sulkily[65] this time, as if each suspected the other of **urging** him to a renewal of the fight. Markey spat out a mouthful of blood from a cut lip; then he **cursed** softly, and picking up his coat and vest, shook off the snow from them in a surprised way, as if their comparative dampness was his only worry in the world.

'Want to come in and wash up[66]?' he asked suddenly.

'No, thanks,' said John. 'I ought to be going home – my wife'll be worried.'

He too picked up his coat and vest and then his overcoat and hat. Soaking wet[67] and dripping with perspiration, it seemed absurd that less than half an hour ago he had been wearing all these clothes.

'Well – good night,' he said hesitantly.

62 very soft; pulp is the inside of fruit or vegetables
63 long thin pieces cut or torn from something
64 *phrase 'playing Indian'*: lying very quietly, as if hunting
65 in a way that shows you are unhappy or angry and not wanting to talk to anyone or be with other people
66 *US phrase 'wash up'*: wash yourself, especially your hands and face
67 extremely wet

Suddenly they walked towards each other and shook hands. It was no perfunctory hand-shake: John Andros's arm went around Markey's shoulder, and he patted him softly on the back for a little while.

'No harm done,' he said brokenly.

'No – you?'

'No, no harm done.'

'Well,' said John Andros after a minute, 'I guess[68] I'll say good night.'

Limping slightly and with his clothes over his arm, John Andros turned away. The moonlight was still bright as he left the dark patch of trampled ground and walked over the intervening lawn. Down at the station, half a mile away, he could hear the rumble of the seven o'clock train.

'But you must have been crazy,' cried Edith brokenly. 'I thought you were going to fix[69] it all up there and shake hands. That's why I went away.'

'Did you want us to fix it up?'

'Of course not, I never want to see them again. But I thought of course that was what you were going to do.' She was touching the **bruises** on his neck and back with iodine[70] as he sat placidly in a hot bath. 'I'm going to get the doctor,' she said insistently. 'You may be hurt internally.'

He shook his head 'Not a chance,' he answered. 'I don't want this to get all over the town.'

'I don't understand yet how it all happened.'

'Neither do I.' He smiled grimly. 'I guess these baby parties are pretty **rough** affairs.'

'Well, one thing – ' suggested Edith hopefully, 'I'm certainly glad we have beef steak in the house for tomorrow's dinner.'

'Why?'

---

68 *informal*: used when you are saying something that you think is probably true or correct
69 *informal*: to find a solution to a situation where things are not working well
70 a dark chemical put on cuts in the skin to prevent infection

'For your eye, of course. Do you know I came within an ace of[71] ordering veal? Wasn't that the luckiest thing?'

Half an hour later, dressed except that his neck would accommodate[72] no collar, John moved his limbs experimentally before the glass[73]. 'I believe I'll get myself in better shape,' he said thoughtfully. 'I must be getting old.'

'You mean so that next time you can beat him?'

'I did beat him,' he announced. 'At least, I beat him as much as he beat me. And there isn't going to be a next time. Don't you go calling people common any more. If you get in any trouble, you just take your coat and go home. Understand?'

'Yes, dear,' she said **meekly**. 'I was very foolish and now I understand.'

Out in the hall, he paused abruptly by the baby's door.

'Is she asleep?'

'Sound asleep[74]. But you can go in and peek at her – just to say good night.'

They **tiptoed** in and bent together over the bed. Little Ede, her cheeks **flushed** with health, her pink hands clasped[75] together, was sleeping soundly in the cool, dark room. John reached over the railing of the bed and passed his hand lightly over the silken[76] hair.

'She's asleep,' he murmured in a puzzled way.

'Naturally, after such an afternoon.'

'Miz Andros,' the coloured[77] maid's stage whisper[78] floated in from the hall. 'Mr and Miz Markey downstairs an' want to see you. Mr Markey he's all cut up in pieces, mam'n. His face look like a roast beef. An' Miz Markey she 'pear mighty mad[79].'

71 *phrase 'came within an ace of'*: almost doing something, or nearly succeeding in doing it
72 provide a place, or room, for something
73 *US*: mirror
74 *phrase 'sound asleep'*: sleeping very well
75 *mainly literary*: held tightly
76 very soft, smooth or shiny
77 *old-fashioned, offensive*: black
78 a way of speaking in which you pretend to talk very quietly but you can be heard by other people
79 she appears to be very angry

'Why, what incomparable nerve[80]!' exclaimed Edith. 'Just tell them we're not home. I wouldn't go down for anything in the world.'

'You most certainly will.' John's voice was hard and set[81].

'What?'

'You'll go down right now, and, what's more, whatever that other woman does, you'll apologize for what you said this afternoon. After that you don't ever have to see her again.'

'Why – John, I can't.'

'You've got to. And just remember that she probably hated to come over here twice as much as you hate to go downstairs.'

'Aren't you coming? Do I have to go alone?'

'I'll be down – in just a minute.'

John Andros waited until she had closed the door behind her; then he reached over into the bed, and picking up his daughter, blankets and all, sat down in the rocking-chair holding her tightly in his arms. She moved a little, and he held his breath, but she was sleeping soundly, and in a moment she was resting quietly in the hollow[82] of his elbow. Slowly he bent his head until his cheek was against her bright hair. 'Dear little girl,' he whispered. 'Dear little girl, dear little girl.'

John Andros knew at length what it was he fought for so savagely that evening. He had it now, he possessed it forever, and for some time he sat there rocking very slowly to and fro in the darkness.

---

80 rude attitude, usually shown by behaviour that makes other people angry
81 not changing, not showing what you really feel
82 an area on someone's body that is slightly lower than the area around it

Post-reading exercises

Understanding the story

1 **Use these questions to help you check that you have understood the story.**

John

1 Where does John work? Where does he live?
2 What happens every afternoon at three o'clock?
3 How old is John? What has his life been like? What is it like now?
4 How does he feel about his daughter?
5 Where is the baby party going to be?
6 What time of year is it?
7 What does John hear as he approaches the Markeys' house?

The party

8 Why does Edith decide to take Ede to the party at five o'clock?
9 How many babies are at the party?
10 Why do Edith and Mrs Markey pretend to like each other?
11 What do the children do when they have finished dancing?
12 When do most parents begin to leave the party?
13 How many children are there at the end of the party?
14 Why does Ede push Billy? Why does he cry?
15 Why do you think Edith laughs?
16 Why does Mrs Markey tell Edith to leave?
17 What does Mrs Markey call Ede? How does Edith react?
18 Why is John angry? Why is Joe angry?

After the party

19 Why does John leave the door open when he leaves the Markeys' house?
20 Where does the fight take place? Why do the men stop fighting?
21 What do the men do before they leave each other?
22 Does John think he won the fight?
23 What does John tell Edith to do in the future?
24 What are John and Edith doing when the Markeys arrive?
25 What does John tell Edith she must do?
26 Why doesn't John go downstairs with his wife?

The Baby Party | 91

Language study

Grammar

Adverbs of manner

Fitzgerald uses a great variety of adverbs of manner in the story to describe actions and develop his characters. Most adverbs of manner answer the question *How?* and are often formed by adding *–ly* to an adjective. Another way of describing actions is by using a prepositional phrase which may or may not contain an adverb, e.g. *with enthusiasm, in surprise, in a puzzled way*.

1 **Which are the adverbs of manner in the extracts below? Which are prepositional phrases?**

1 Edith Andros, calculating shrewdly that the new dress would stand out more sensationally against vestments already rumpled …
2 Billy Markey … held the toy closely in his arms.
3 Ede stood regarding him with inscrutable eyes …
4 Grown-up Edith looked at her watch again, this time impatiently.
5 Ede had obtained Billy's teddy-bear by pulling it forcibly from his arms, and on Billy's attempt to recover it, she had pushed him casually to the floor.
6 'It's swollen already,' he said with a note of reproof in his voice.
7 Little Ede meanwhile had been looking at her mother curiously.
8 Pressing her handkerchief to her mouth she giggled irrepressibly.

2 **Adverbs of manner are often used after verbs such as *say, answer, cry* etc. Look at these examples from the text. Underline the verb and adverb.**

he said jovially [page 81]
said Ede emphatically [page 82]
she whispered perfunctorily [page 82]
cried Mrs Markey frantically [page 83]
exclaimed Edith brokenly [page 84]
objected Markey hurriedly [page 84]
demanded John abruptly [page 84]
burst out Markey violently [page 85]

3 **Make adverbs from the adjectives in brackets and write them in the correct place in the sentence. There may be more than one correct answer.**

1 'I must be getting old,' said John. (thoughtful)
2 'Baby parties are rough affairs,' he said. (grim)
3 Joe asked John if he wanted to go into the house. (sudden)
4 Markey cried that he wouldn't go on with the fight. (thick)
5 Mrs Markey picked Billy up from the sofa. (quick)
6 'Please go home!' she broke out. (angry)
7 Edith looked at her little girl in her new pink dress. (proud)
8 All the children were in motion running to and from their mothers. (continual)
9 John passed his hand over his child's head. (light)
10 He sat in the darkness rocking to and fro. (slow)

Present participles in adverbial clauses

Fitzgerald often uses phrases containing present participles, to add extra information or describe actions that take place at the same time or very close to each other.

Look at these examples from the story:

Increasing his gait he came in sight of his own house [page 78].
Accepting a cup of tea she took a seat with two other ladies on the divan [page 79].
Taking up her daughter in her arms, his wife stepped outside [page 86].
Then, staggering to their feet, they looked at each other like two drunken men [page 87].

Notice how the subject of the main clause is also the subject of the participle.

The example below is grammatically incorrect because the subject of the participle is *petrol*, which is becoming more expensive, and the subject of the main clause is *people*.

Becoming more expensive every day, people can no longer afford to pay for petrol.

4 How could you express the above sentence correctly?

5 Rewrite these sentences using a present participle and making any necessary changes.

1 She pressed her handkerchief to her mouth and laughed uncontrollably.
   Pressing her handkerchief to her mouth, she laughed uncontrollably.
2 As he made his way up the steps, he whistled cheerfully.
3 She took the toy from the little boy and ignored his protests.
4 John took off his jacket and then punched Joe on the nose.

5 I kept my eye on the clock and dialled Susan's number.
6 'I don't want to go!' the child cried and hit out at his father.
7 He was sweating profusely. He dragged the heavy box along the floor.
8 They barked loudly. The dogs made a lot of noise as they ran round the garden.

Literary analysis
Plot
1 What are the first four paragraphs about? Why are they important?
2 Where is John when we first meet him in the story? What is he doing?
3 When John arrives at the party, what is happening?
4 What events take place at the party while John is on his way there?
5 Which adult characters does the author focus on at the party? Why?
6 Why do you think Joe and John have a fight?
7 Who do you think is to blame for all the trouble?
8 Read the last two paragraphs of the story again. How would you interpret the sentence: *John Andros knew at length what it was he had fought for so savagely that evening* [page 90]?

Character
9 Complete these details about John Andros:
Age:
Work:
Health:
Financial position:
Personality:
Mood before the party:
10 What *chiefly interests* John about his daughter? Why do you think this is?
11 How does John sometimes feel when his daughter behaves badly? How does he feel afterwards?
12 How would you describe John's wife? Who is the dominant partner in their marriage?
13 What does John's wife think of Mrs Markey? Do you agree with her?
14 What kind of person is Joe Markey? What do you think his relationship with John will be like from now on?

15 What do you think happens when John and his wife finally speak to the Markeys after the party? Will their relationship change in any way?

Narration

16 How important is dialogue in the story?
17 Fitzgerald's writing is sometimes described as 'bitter-sweet'. Why do you think this is?
18 There are several episodes in the story that are important, for example, the incident between Ede and Billy; the argument between Edith and Mrs Markey. Which other episodes are important? Why?
19 Some of the story is quite humorous, for example the description of the babies at the party. Which other parts of the narrative contain humour?
20 There is a balance between third-person narrative and dialogue in the story. Find examples of this. What effect does it have?
21 Who does Fitzgerald identify with most in the story? How do you know?
22 Do you think the descriptions of the party, the fight and what happens afterwards are exaggerated? Why/why not?

Atmosphere

23 In the first part of the story, John is in a good mood. How does the author convey this?
24 How does Fitzgerald convey the increasing activity of the babies at the party?
25 What happens after Ede gives her *infectious laugh*? How does Fitzgerald convey the atmosphere of rising hysteria?
26 The fight between John and Joe takes place in silence. What effect does this have? When they stop fighting and begin to talk, how does the atmosphere change?
27 What kind of atmosphere is conveyed by the description of Ede asleep at the end of the story?

Style

28 When Fitzgerald describes John, he sometimes uses a lyrical, poetic style:

The dark trumpets of oblivion were less loud at the patter of his child's feet …[page 76].

… his life had been a series of struggles up a series of rugged hills … [page 76].

… he cherished less than the usual number of illusions … [page 76].

Can you find other examples of this kind of style?

29 Fitzgerald sometimes uses exaggerated or overblown language to obtain a comic effect:

Edith Andros, calculating shrewdly that the new dress would stand out more sensationally against vestments already rumpled … (i.e. that her baby would look better than the others after they had got dirty at the party).

Look again at the paragraph that starts *An hour passed* [page 79]. Which words or phrases suggest that the author is comparing the children's activity to a military operation?

Guidance to the above literary terms, answer keys to all the exercises and activities, plus a wealth of other reading-practice material, can be found on the student's section of the Macmillan Readers website at: www.macmillanenglish.com/readers.

You Were Perfectly Fine
by Dorothy Parker

About the author

Dorothy Parker was born Dorothy Rothschild in 1893 in New Jersey, in the USA. Her mother, who died when Dorothy was very young, was of Scottish descent. Her father was a Jewish garment-manufacturer[1].

Dorothy grew up in New York City, where she attended a Catholic convent school, and then Miss Dana's School in Morristown, New Jersey. In 1916, she sold some of her poetry to *Vogue* magazine, where she later worked, writing copy for fashion photographs and drawings. She then became a drama critic for another magazine, *Vanity Fair*. At this time, she married Edwin Pond Parker II. They were divorced some years later, but Dorothy continued to use his surname.

Dorothy was a key member of the Algonquin Round Table. This was a group of journalists, editors, actors and press agents who met regularly for lunch at the Algonquin Hotel, New York City, over a period of about eight years, starting in 1919. The magazine *The New Yorker* was also founded at the hotel. From 1926 until 1955, Dorothy's short stories were published at irregular intervals in this magazine. Many of them are based on incidents and conversations that took place at the Algonquin.

In 1926, a book of Dorothy's poems was published under the title *Enough Rope*, and it became a best-seller. Parker released two more volumes of verse, *Sunset Gun* (1927) and *Death and Taxes* (1931), along with the short-story collections *Laments for the Living* (1930) and *After Such Pleasures* (1933).

In 1934, Dorothy married the actor-writer Alan Campbell who was 11 years younger than her. They went to Hollywood as a screenwriting team and bought a farm in Pennsylvania. Dorothy became pregnant at the age of 42, but she lost the baby in the third month of pregnancy. Dorothy and Campbell were divorced in 1947 and remarried in 1950. Their marriage was always difficult and they spent long periods living apart. Campbell died in 1963 and Dorothy returned to New York. Her

1 someone whose job is to make clothes

last important piece of writing was a play, *The Ladies of the Corridor*, an account of life in a New York residential hotel. By this time she was drinking heavily and in 1967 she died alone in a hotel room.

Dorothy Parker is remembered for her cynical, urbane humour and sharp observations of human behaviour. Her witticisms are often quoted, and theatrical dramatisations of her work are still very popular.

About the story

You Were Perfectly Fine was published in 1929, the same year that Parker won the O Henry Award for the best short story of the year, with *Big Blonde*. Her writing was criticised by some as 'flapper verse', a style associated with over-confident young women making fun of conventional social and sexual rules. However, Parker's short stories, though often witty, are also spare and incisive, and more bittersweet than comic.

The economy of this story, and its amusing conversation, make it perfect for theatrical performance.

Background information

The 1920s in the USA

The decade of the 1920s is sometimes known as 'the Roaring Twenties' or 'the Jazz Age', and is often described as a time of carefree abandon and excess in all things. This is only partly true, and did not apply to all sectors of society. After the First World War, there was a period of prosperity and economic expansion in the USA. Production increased and more people were able to afford things like refrigerators, cars and washing machines. There was a demand, too, for more entertainment, and the number of music bars, theatres and cinemas grew. Social changes meant that women were freer than before, and this was reflected in their dress and speech. Dorothy Parker was a 'modern' woman who did what she wanted and spoke her mind freely.

Prohibition

In the USA, 'Prohibition' refers to the period from 1920 to 1933 when the manufacture and sale of alcohol was prohibited by law. It was thought that if people did not drink alcohol, they would work harder and there would be less crime. However, the law was not a success. Criminal gangs sold alcohol on the black market, and there was violence between the different gangs. Many people ignored the law and drank anyway.

In the story, set in the late 1920s, the young man is suffering after drinking heavily the night before. Dorothy Parker herself drank heavily, and the meetings of the Round Table were certainly not alcohol-free. *You Were Perfectly Fine* is essentially a critical observation of the negative effects of heavy drinking.

Summary

It may help you to know something about what happens in the story before you read it. Don't worry, this summary does *not* tell you how the story ends!

The story is based on a conversation between a young man and woman.

Both have attended the same dinner in a hotel restaurant the night before, but the young man cannot remember much about it because he drank too much. Today, he feels terrible and asks the girl how he behaved at the dinner. The girl tells him that he was *perfectly fine*, but gradually reveals various events that took place which make the young man feel ashamed of himself. Finally, the girl describes how they both went for a taxi ride together at the end of the evening. Her description of what happened in the taxi leaves the young man feeling worse than ever.

Pre-reading exercises

Key vocabulary

This section will help you familiarise yourself with some of the more specific vocabulary used in the story. You may want to use it to help you before you start reading, or as a revision exercise after you have finished the story.

Exclamations

Peter, the young man in the story, is sorry that he drank too much the night before, and the girl tries to reassure him that his behaviour was not as bad as he thinks. They preface many of their comments with different expressions showing repentance or reassurance.

1 Look at the following exclamations. Which do you think are made by the man and which by the woman?

a) Oh, dear, oh, dear, oh, dear.
b) Oh, goodness ... everybody was feeling pretty high.
c) Good heavens, no ... Everyone thought you were terribly funny.
d) Why, you didn't do a thing ...
e) My, you were funny.
f) Dear God. What'll I ever do?

Expressions

The young couple in the story use a number of informal or colloquial expressions.

2 Match the expressions in bold below with their definitions in the right-hand column. Then read the story and check your answers.

1 I kept trying to **make it** (out of bed).
2 **The hair of the dog** (in the story, *mastiff*).
3 I'm **through**.
4 I did think you were just a little **tight**.
5 You **made too much fuss** over her.
6 Was I **making a pass at** her?
7 I **haven't got a care in the world**.
8 I'm **sitting pretty**.
9 I'm **off the stuff for life**.
10 I **feel a collapse coming on**.
11 I **made such a fool of myself**.

a) without worries
b) in an advantageous position
c) paid excessive attention to
d) behaved badly, stupidly
e) never going to do something ever again
f) I think I'm going to collapse
g) drunk
h) have decided to stop doing something
i) manage to do something
j) making an amorous advance
k) an alcoholic drink taken to cure a hangover

100 | *You Were Perfectly Fine*

US English

The writer uses some words and expressions that are mainly used only in the USA.

3 Look at the words below and complete the sentences in British English.

angry	go and join	suppose	finished	go and make
joking	pavement	tie	excellent	

US English	British English
1 I'm **through** with drinking.	I'm .... with drinking.
2 I must have been **dandy**.	I must have been ....
3 Is everybody **sore** at me?	Is everybody .... with me?
4 You were only **fooling**.	You were only ....
5 You didn't like his **necktie**.	You didn't like his ....
6 You sat down on the **sidewalk**.	You sat down on the ....
7 I **guess** it must have been.	I .... it must have been.
8 I'll **go make** you a drink.	I'll .... you a drink.
9 I'd better **go join** a monastery.	I'd better .... a monastery.

Main themes

Before you read the story, you may want to think about some of its main themes. The questions will help you think about the story as you are reading it for the first time. There is more discussion of the main themes in the *Literary analysis* section after the story.

Male/female relationships in New York society in the 1920s

At this time, women in the USA were achieving greater equality with men. This was the time of the 'flapper' or young woman who cut her hair short, wore short dresses, smoked, drank and went out to parties. It is not clear if the woman in the story is of this type, but it is certainly possible. She was at a dinner the night before with a mixture of people, married and unmarried, they all drank or did not mind if others drank, and, as far as we know, she was not officially escorted by a man.

4 As you read the story, ask yourself:

a) Do the men and the women in the story seem to have equal status?
b) Who has greater control over the situation, Peter or the young woman? Why?

The place of alcohol in society

The conversation in the story revolves around the fact that Peter drank too much the previous evening, and now, feels terrible and cannot remember much of what happened. At the time, drinking alcohol was officially prohibited by the government, and yet it is obvious that it continued, even in public places, such as the hotel or restaurant where the previous night's dinner has taken place.

The conversation between Peter and his 'girlfriend' seems to take place in an apartment and, again, there is abundant alcohol available, since she offers more than once to make him a drink.

5 As you read the story, ask yourself:

a) What seems to be the general attitude of the people in the story towards alcohol?
b) How is the young woman in the story using alcohol to manipulate Pete?

★ ★ ★ ★

You Were Perfectly Fine

by Dorothy Parker

The pale young man eased himself carefully into the low chair, and rolled his head to the side, so that the cool **chintz** comforted his cheek and temple.

"Oh, dear," he said. "Oh, dear, oh, dear, oh, dear. Oh."

The clear-eyed girl, sitting light and erect on the couch, smiled brightly at him.

"Not feeling so well today?" she said.

"Oh, I'm great," he said. "Corking[2], I am. Know what time I got up? Four o'clock this afternoon, sharp. I kept trying to make it, and every time I took my head off the pillow, it would roll under the bed. This isn't my head I've got on now. I think this is something that used to belong to Walt Whitman[3]. Oh, dear, oh, dear, oh, dear."

"Do you think maybe a drink would make you feel better?" she said.

"The hair of the **mastiff** that bit me?" he said. "Oh, no, thank you. Please never speak of anything like that again. I'm through. I'm all, all through. Look at that hand; steady as a **hummingbird**. Tell me, was I very terrible last night?"

"Oh, goodness," she said, "everybody was feeling pretty high. You were all right."

"Yeah," he said. "I must have been dandy. Is everybody sore at me?"

"Good heavens, no," she said. "Everyone thought you were terribly funny. Of course, Jim Pierson was a little stuffy[4], there, for a minute at dinner. But people sort of held him back in his chair, and got him calmed down. I don't think anybody at the other tables noticed it at all. Hardly anybody."

---

2 *old-fashioned*: wonderful, splendid
3 influential American poet and humanist (1819–1892)
4 *informal*: criticising anyone whose behaviour is unusual

"He was going to sock[5] me?" he said. "Oh, Lord. What did I do to him?"

"Why, you didn't do a thing," she said. "You were perfectly fine. But you know how silly Jim gets, when he thinks anybody is making too much fuss over Elinor."

"Was I making a pass at Elinor?" he said. "Did I do that?"

"Of course you didn't" she said. "You were only fooling, that's all. She thought you were awfully amusing. She was having a marvellous time. She only got a little tiny bit annoyed just once, when you poured the **clam**-juice down her back."

"My God," he said. "Clam-juice down that back. And every vertebra a little Cabot[6]. Dear God. What'll I ever do?"

"Oh, she'll be all right," she said. "Just send her some flowers, or something. Don't worry about it. It isn't anything."

"No, I won't worry," he said. "I haven't got a care in the world. I'm sitting pretty. Oh, dear, oh, dear. Did I do any other fascinating tricks at dinner?"

"You were fine," she said. "Don't be so foolish about it. Everybody was crazy about you. The maitre d'hotel was a little worried because you wouldn't stop singing, but he really didn't mind. All he said was, he was afraid they'd close the place again, if there was so much noise. But he didn't care a bit, himself. I think he loved seeing you have such a good time. Oh, you were just singing away, there, for about an hour. It wasn't so terribly loud, at all."

"So I sang," he said. "That must have been a treat. I sang."

"Don't you remember?" she said. "You just sang one song after another. Everybody in the place was listening. They loved it. Only you kept insisting that you wanted to sing some song about some kind of fusiliers[7] or other, and everybody kept shushing[8] you, and you'd keep trying to start it again. You were wonderful. We were all trying to make you stop singing for a minute, and eat

5 *informal*: to hit someone or something with a lot of force
6 probably referring to John Cabot the Italian-born explorer who discovered Newfoundland and Nova Scotia in North America. Peter is comparing Elinor's vertebrae to small islands
7 soldiers armed with a gun
8 telling someone to be quiet

something, but you wouldn't hear of it. My, you were funny."

"Didn't I eat any dinner?" he said.

"Oh, not a thing," she said. "Every time the waiter would offer you something, you'd give it right back to him, because you said that he was your long-lost brother, changed in the **cradle** by a gypsy band, and that anything you had was his. You had him simply roaring at you."

"I bet I did," he said. "I bet I was comical. Society's Pet, I must have been. And what happened then, after my **overwhelming** success with the waiter?"

"Why, nothing much," she said. "You took a sort of dislike to some old man with white hair, sitting across the room, because you didn't like his necktie and you wanted to tell him about it. But we got you out, before he got really mad."

"Oh, we got out," he said. "Did I walk?"

"Walk! Of course you did," she said. "You were absolutely all right. There was that **nasty** stretch of ice on the **sidewalk**, and you did sit down awfully hard, you poor dear. But good heavens, that might have happened to anybody."

"Oh, sure," he said. "Louisa Alcott[9] or anybody. So I fell down on the sidewalk. That would explain what's the matter with my —Yes. I see. And then what, if you don't mind?"

"Ah, now, Peter!" she said. "You can't sit there and say you don't remember what happened after that! I did think that maybe you were just a little tight at dinner – oh, you were perfectly all right, and all that, but I did know you were feeling pretty gay[10]. But you were so serious, from the time you fell down – I never knew you to be that way. Don't you know, how you told me I had never seen your real self before? Oh, Peter, I just couldn't bear it, if you didn't remember that lovely long ride we took together in the taxi! Please, you do remember that, don't you? I think it would simply kill me, if you didn't."

"Oh, yes," he said. "Riding in the taxi. Oh, yes, sure. Pretty long ride, hmm?"

---

9 US novelist, most famous for *Little Women*, a novel about four sisters, thought by some people to be over-sentimental and moralistic (1832–1888)

10 happy, cheerful; here, as the result of drinking

"Round and round and round the park," she said. "Oh, and the trees were shining so in the moonlight. And you said you never knew before that you really had a **soul**."

"Yes," he said. "I said that. That was me."

"You said such lovely, lovely things," she said. "And I'd never known, all this time, how you had been feeling about me, and I'd never dared to let you see how I felt about you. And then last night – oh, Peter dear, I think that taxi ride was the most important thing that ever happened to us in our lives."

"Yes," he said. "I guess it must have been."

"And we're going to be so happy," she said. "Oh, I just want to tell everybody! But I don't know – I think maybe it would be sweeter to keep it all to ourselves."

"I think it would be," he said.

"Isn't it lovely?" she said.

"Yes," he said. "Great."

"Lovely!" she said.

"Look here," he said, "do you mind if I have a drink? I mean, just medicinally, you know. I'm off the stuff[11] for life, so help me. But I think I feel a collapse coming on."

"Oh, I think it would do you good," she said. "You poor boy, it's a shame you feel so awful. I'll go make you a whisky and soda."

"Honestly," he said, "I don't see how you could ever want to speak to me again, after I made such a fool of myself, last night. I think I'd better go join a monastery in Tibet."

"You crazy idiot!" she said. "As if I could ever let you go away now! Stop talking like that. You were perfectly fine."

She jumped up from the couch, kissed him quickly on the forehead, and ran out of the room.

The pale young man looked after her and shook his head long and slowly, then dropped it in his **damp** and trembling hands.

"Oh, dear," he said. "Oh, dear, oh, dear, oh, dear."

---

11 material, substance; here, referring to alcohol

Post-reading exercises

Understanding the story

1 Use these questions to help you check that you have understood the story.

1. How does the young man feel at the beginning of the story? How do you know?
2. How do you think the young woman feels? What evidence is there for your opinion?
3. What time did the young man get up? Why?
4. What does the young man want to know about the previous evening?
5. According to the young woman, why was Jim Pierson *a little stuffy*?
6. Why was Elinor *a tiny little bit annoyed*?
7. How long was the young man singing? How did the maitre d'hotel react?
8. Why didn't the young man eat anything?
9. Why was the young man taken out of the hotel?
10. What happened on the sidewalk?
11. Where did Peter and the young woman go in the taxi? What happened in the taxi?
12. How does the young woman feel about what happened in the taxi?
13. Why do you think Peter asks for a drink?
14. How do you think Peter feels after the young woman leaves the room?

Language study

Grammar

Ellipsis

In informal spoken English, we often omit words at the beginning of sentences if the meaning is clear from the context.

Look at these examples from the story:

Not feeling so well today? [page 103]
Know what time I got up? [page 103]
Pretty long ride, hmm? [page 105]

1 Complete the sentences below so that they mean the same as the examples on page 107.

Aren't .... ?
Do .... ?
It was .... ?

2 Write the phrases below as complete sentences.

1 Seen Sandra?
2 Nobody at home today, I'm afraid.
3 Anybody want more food?
4 You be here tomorrow?
5 Your father got a car?
6 Dora coming to the party?

Fronting in informal speech

In informal spoken English, as in literary English, it is quite common to begin an affirmative sentence with the object or complement, in order to give this part more emphasis.

3 Look at these examples from the story. Who is speaking? What would the normal word order be?

"*Corking, I am.*" [page 103]
"*Society's Pet, I must have been.*" [page 105]

4 Rewrite these sentences so that the object or complement is given more emphasis.

1 We had an excellent dinner last night.
   Excellent dinner we had last night.
2 That was a great concert!
3 They were furious with me.
4 He's my favourite singer.
5 That must have been awful.
6 She's feeling terrible.

The use of *get*

Get is one of the most common verbs in spoken English. It has several different meanings. Look at the different uses of *get* in these examples from the story.

This isn't my head I've got on now. (wearing)
But people ... got him calmed down. (managed)

She only got a little tiny bit annoyed. (became)
I haven't got a care in the world. (don't have)
But we got you out, before he got really mad. (take; became)

5 **Rewrite the sentences above using the words in brackets and making any other necessary changes.**

6 **Rewrite these sentences using an appropriate form of *get*.**

1 I don't think he received my letter.
2 She'll come and collect you from the airport.
3 I realised later that I hadn't understood the joke.
4 Tom has finally had his car fixed.
5 When are you going to have your hair cut?
6 Make her stop singing in the shower, will you?

Literary analysis

Plot

1 The girl describes the previous evening to Peter. What were the main events? Make a list:
   – Peter poured clam-juice down Elinor's back.
   – Jim was going to hit Peter but …
   – The maitre d'hotel …
2 What was the most important event of the evening, according to the young woman? Do you think Peter remembers anything about it?
3 What is the young woman referring to when she says *maybe it would be sweeter to keep it all to ourselves*? Why do you think she says this? Does Peter agree with her? Why?
4 What do you think will happen now?

Character

5 How are the young man and woman described at the beginning of the story? What do these descriptions tell us?
6 How would you describe the young woman? Why do you think the author does not give her a name?
7 How would you describe Peter? Do you think this is the first time he has drunk too much? What evidence is there?
8 Which other people are mentioned in the story? What is their relationship with the two main characters?

Narration

9. Do you believe the young woman's version of what happened the night before? Why?
10. Do you think that Peter believes what the young woman tells him? Why?
11. What is the main type of narration in the story: description or direct speech? What effect does this have?
12. Think about how the story would have been told from the point of view of Jim Pierson, Elinor, the maitre d'hotel, or the waiter. How would it be different?

Atmosphere

13. What elements contribute to the humour of the conversation? Think about, for example, the order in which events are told, and the details provided.
14. How does the author give us an idea of the lifestyle of her main characters? Think about the hotel, the meal, the taxi, drink etc.
15. Is the atmosphere of the story light-hearted or is there a dark side to it? Why do you think this?

Style

16. Read the beginning of the story as far as *"Not feeling so well today?" she said*. How does the author convey the contrasting physical states of her main characters?
17. Most of the story consists of direct speech. Who speaks the most? Who asks the most questions? Why?
18. Notice how Parker mostly uses 'he said' or 'she said' without any adverbs or explanatory phrases. Why do you think she does this?
19. Notice how the young woman 'consoles' Peter, but at the same time suggests that he behaved very badly e.g.:

    "I don't think anybody at the other tables noticed it at all. Hardly anybody." [page 103]

    "She was having a marvellous time. She only got a little tiny bit annoyed just once, when you poured the clam-juice down her back." [page 104]

    Can you find any more examples of this mixture of reassurance and revelation? What effect does it have?

20 This story is sometimes performed as a play. Try reading part of it aloud. Do you think it would be effective as a play?

Guidance to the above literary terms, answer keys to all the exercises and activities plus a wealth of other reading-practice material can be found on the student's section of the Macmillan Readers website at www.macmillanenglish.com/readers.

The Romantic
by Patricia Highsmith

About the author

Patricia Highsmith was an American mystery writer, but her works were especially successful in Europe. She had roots in Europe – her father was of German descent, and her maternal grandmother was Scottish. She was born Mary Patricia Plangman near Fort Worth, Texas in 1921, but grew up in New York City. Her parents were both commercial artists. They divorced before she was born and she did not meet her father until she was 12 years old. She took the surname Highsmith from her stepfather. Highsmith had an intense and difficult relationship with her mother, which upset her all her life, and she was closer to her grandmother, who took care of her when she was a little girl.

Highsmith was educated at Julia Richmond High School, New York City, and Barnard College. She edited the school magazine and decided at the age of 16 to become a writer. After leaving college, she spent some time working on storylines and scripts for comic books.

Her first novel, *Strangers on a Train*, was published in 1950. It was about two men who meet on a train and decide to 'exchange' murders. The book was turned into a film by the director Alfred Hitchcock, famous for making thrillers that were full of suspense.

Highsmith is best known for her 'Ripley' novels, psychological thrillers which feature her amoral hero, Tom Ripley. *The Talented Mr Ripley* was her third novel and was awarded the Edgar Allen Poe Scroll[1] by the organisation the Mystery Writers of America. The main character, Ripley, is a thief and a killer, yet Highsmith manages to make his actions seem almost normal and engage the reader's sympathy. The Ripley saga inspired various films, among them *The American Friend* (1977) directed by Wim Wenders, and *The Talented Mr Ripley*, directed by Anthony Minghella (1999).

Highsmith never married and lived for much of her life in Europe, particularly in England, France and Switzerland. She was a talented painter and carpenter. She could also be eccentric[2]: a neighbour of hers

1 a famous literary award
2 someone who behaves in strange and unusual ways

in France once told her that he had heard a lot of banging noises during the night and asked her if everything was all right. She explained that in one of her novels, Ripley has to make a coffin for one of his victims and she wanted to see how long it would have taken him, so she made the coffin herself and timed the operation.

Highsmith spent her final years in an isolated house near Locarno, on the Swiss-Italian border. She died in Switzerland in 1995. Her reputation is assured through the Ripley books, but she also left behind some excellent short stories, a book for younger readers, and some interesting non-fiction works on the art of writing.

About the story

The Romantic was first published in *Cosmopolitan*, London, in 1983. It later formed part of the collection *Mermaids on the Golf Course*, published in 1985.

Background information

New York City

The story takes place in New York City where the main character Isabel lives and works. Famous landmarks are mentioned, such as Central Park, the biggest park in the city, and the Metropolitan Museum, a large museum full of varied exhibits.

New York City consists of several areas, among them the island of Manhattan, Queens and Brooklyn, all referred to in the story. The streets of New York are laid out to a grid[3] plan and are named according to their orientation and number. Isabel lives on West 55th Street. She goes to a bar on Sixth Avenue in the *upper 50s*. There are references to *downtown*, the central business and shopping area of the city, and *uptown*, the area furthest away from the centre.

Romantic fiction

Isabel reads a lot of *romance novels*. This type of novel became popular in the UK and the USA around 100 years ago, and is still a favourite with readers today. In the USA, the demand for romantic fiction reached its height during the economic Depression of the 1930s. Such novels were particularly popular among women. Reading the stories helped them escape the harsh reality of their lives.

3 a pattern of straight lines that cross each other to form squares

In the story, Isabel borrows some of her books from the public library and also buys a few in paperback. Paperback versions of romance novels are published in great numbers today. Some features of the genre have been modernised to suit today's reader, but the basic plot – a hero and a heroine, separated by fate and circumstances, who eventually conquer all problems and come together in a 'happy ending' is the same now as it was a 100 years ago.

Summary

It may help you to know something about what happens in the story before you read it. Don't worry, this summary does *not* tell you how the story ends!

Isabel Crane is 23 years old and works as secretary and typist for a company in New York City. She is an only child (i.e. she has no brothers or sisters) and an orphan (i.e. she has no parents). Her father died when she was 19 and her mother a few years later. Isabel went straight from school to work in order to help with the family finances.

After her mother's death, Isabel looks forward to a more exciting social life, but nothing much happens. In the evenings, she reads romance novels, which she has loved since the age of 14.

One day, a handsome man, Dudley Hall, appears at the office and Isabel helps him. Over the next few days, he appears again on several occasions. When his business is finished, Dudley asks Isabel to go for a meal with him the following evening. They arrange to meet at half past six.

On the night of the date, Isabel dresses with care and goes to the restaurant. She sits in the bar and orders a drink. Dudley does not appear. At five to eight, Isabel goes home.

The next day, Dudley telephones and says he was in a meeting and could not get away. He apologises but does not ask Isabel for another date.

Eva Rosenau, a friend of Isabel's mother, visits Isabel and invites her for Sunday dinner. Isabel accepts, but on Sunday morning, she telephones Eva and tells her that she isn't coming because she has some work to do for the office.

That evening, Isabel dresses up and goes to a bar by herself. She orders a drink and pretends that she is waiting for someone. After

45 minutes, she leaves and goes home.

Isabel's 'fantasy dates' become a regular feature of her life and soon she is going out by herself twice a week. People comment on the fact that she looks happier.

Two weeks before her vacation, Isabel receives a telephone call from Wilbur Miller, a client, who wants to take her out to dinner. They make a date for the following Friday.

Isabel arrives at the restaurant on Friday evening. She stands outside, looking for Wilbur among the passers-by, but then she reflects that he is probably inside, waiting for her ...

Pre-reading exercises

Key vocabulary

This section will help you familiarise yourself with some of the more specific vocabulary used in the story. You may want to use it to help you before you start reading, or as a revision exercise after you have finished the story.

Vocabulary connected with romantic relationships

1 Look at the vocabulary and definitions in the box below, and then use the words and phrases to complete the paragraph that follows.

> **to ask someone for a date** to ask someone to go out with you
> **to have a steady boyfriend/girlfriend** to have a romantic relationship with someone for a long time
> **to become engaged to someone** to formally promise to marry someone
> **to have a fiancé/to be engaged** to have a person you have formally agreed to marry
> **to get married to someone** to marry, to become someone's husband or wife
> **to pick someone up** to try and establish contact with someone in order to have a relationship with them
> **to play it cool** to behave calmly and unemotionally so that people don't know what you are feeling or thinking
> **to have a drink on someone** to be invited by someone to have a drink
> **to stand someone up** to not come to meet someone that you have arranged to meet, especially someone you are having or starting a romantic relationship with
> **to have an affair with someone** to have a romantic relationship with someone

Sara had not had a .... relationship for a long time. All her friends had already got .... or were .... and planned to marry in the near future. Sara knew she could have an .... whenever she wanted with James, but he was married and there would be no future in it.

Then one day, sitting alone at the bar of the hotel, Sara met Tom. He tried to .... almost immediately and asked her to .... on him. Sara tried not to look too interested, but she found it hard to .... because Tom was very attractive.

They arranged to have dinner together the following week. Sara was devastated when Tom failed to appear. It was the first time in her life that anyone had ....

Main themes

Before you read the story, you may want to think about some of its main themes. The questions will help you think about the story as you are reading it for the first time. There is more discussion of the main themes in the *Literary analysis* section after the story.

Madness

Highsmith was very interested in human psychology and what constituted 'normal' behaviour. Her characters often lead double lives: one 'normal' life which they show to the world and another, darker, more mysterious life which is usually hidden.

2 As you read the story, ask yourself:

a) How normal is Isabel's behaviour?
b) Are there any signs that she may be going mad?

Romance

Isabel reads a lot of romance novels. These novels follow a pattern: the hero and heroine have to overcome a series of obstacles before the traditional 'happy ending' when they are finally united in love and/or marriage.

3 As you read the story, ask yourself:

a) How far is Isabel's behaviour affected by these novels?
b) Can Isabel always distinguish between fantasy and reality?

Loneliness

Many of Highsmith's characters suffer from loneliness or alienation. Isabel has suffered the loss of both her parents in a short time.

The story is written from the point of view of Isabel. When talking about Isabel's feelings and thoughts, Highsmith sometimes uses very long, multiple-clause sentences in this story, such as this one, in the opening paragraph:

Boyfriends and parties had been minimal, and she had been in love only once, she thought, or maybe one and a half times, if she counted what she now considered a minor hang-up at twenty on a married man, who had been quite willing to start an affair, but Isabel had held back, thinking it would lead nowhere.

The length of the sentences reflect the dialogue Isabel has with herself, an internal conversation that continues at all times, which – perhaps – helps to protect her from loneliness.

4 As you read the story, ask yourself:

a) Is Isabel's bereavement the main cause of her increasingly strange behaviour?

b) Is Isabel responsible for her growing isolation?

★ ★ ★ ★

The Romantic

by Patricia Highsmith

When Isabel Crane's mother died after an illness that had kept her in and out of hospitals for five years and finally at home, Isabel had thought that her life would change dramatically. Isabel was twenty-three, and since eighteen, when many young people embarked on four happy years at college, Isabel had stayed at home, with a job, of course, to help with finances. Boyfriends and parties had been minimal, and she had been in love only once, she thought, or maybe one and a half times, if she counted what she now considered a minor **hang-up** at twenty on a married man, who had been quite willing to start an affair, but Isabel had held back, thinking it would lead nowhere. The first young man hadn't liked her enough, but he had **lingered** longer, in Isabel's affections, more than a year.

Yet six weeks after her mother's funeral, Isabel found that her life had not changed much after all. She had imagined parties, liveliness in the apartment, young people. Well, that could come, of course. She had lost contact with a lot of her old high-school[4] friends, because they had got married, moved, and now she didn't know where to reach most of them. But the world was full of people.

Even the apartment on West 55th Street had not changed much, though she remembered, while her mother had still been alive, imagining changing the boring dubonnet-and-cream[5] coloured curtains, now limp with age, and getting rid of the nutty little "settles"[6] as her mother had called them, which took up space and looked like 1940 or worse. These were armless wooden seats without backs, which no one ever sat on, because they

---

4 US: in the USA, a school for children between the ages of 14 and 18
5 Dubonnet is a wine-based drink of a reddish colour
6 a long wooden chair for two or three people

looked fragile, rather like little tables. Then there were the old books, not even classics, which filled more than half of the two bookcases (otherwise filled with better books or at least newer books), which Isabel imagined **chucking**, thereby[7] leaving space for the occasional objet d'art[8] or statuette[9] or something, such as she had seen in magazine photographs of attractive living-room interiors. But after weeks and weeks, little of this had been done, certainly not the curtains, and Isabel found that she couldn't shed[10] even one settle, because nobody she knew wanted one. She had given away her mother's clothes and handbags to the Salvation Army[11].

Isabel was a secretary-typist at Weiler and Diggs, an agency that handled office space in the Manhattan and Queens areas. She had learned typing and steno[12] in her last year at high school. There were four other secretaries, but only Isabel and two others, Priscilla (Prissy) and Valerie, took turns as receptionist at the lobby[13] desk for a week, because they were younger and prettier than the other two secretaries. It was Prissy, who was very outspoken, who had said this one day, and Isabel thought it was true.

Prissy Kupperman was going to be married in a few months, and she had met her fiancé one day when she had been at the front desk, and he had walked in. "Reception" was a great place to meet people, men on the way up, all the girls said. Eighty per cent of Weiler and Diggs' clientele was male. A girl could put herself out a little, escort the man to the office he wanted, and when he left, ask him if his visit had been successful and say, "My name is Prissy (or whatever) and if you need to get a message through or any special service, I'll see that it's done."

7 *old-fashioned, literary, formal:* thus, in this way
8 *French:* an object that is mostly for decoration but is also considered to be a work of art
9 a small human or animal image that is made of stone, wood, metal, etc
10 get rid of something that is not wanted or is no longer necessary
11 an international organisation that teaches Christianity and helps people with problems
12 *abbreviation of 'stenography':* a system of writing very quickly using special signs
13 *mainly US:* the area just inside the entrance to a hotel, theatre or other large building

Prissy had done something along these lines the day her Jeff had walked in.

Valerie, only twenty and a more **lightweight** type than Prissy, had had several dates with men she had met at work, but she wasn't ready for marriage, she said, and besides had a steady boyfriend whom she preferred. Isabel had tried the same tactics, escorting[14] young men to the office they wanted, but this so far had never led to a date. Isabel would dearly have loved 'a second encounter[15]' as she termed it to herself, with some of these young men who might have phoned back and asked to speak with Isabel. She imagined being invited out to dinner, possibly at a place where they had dancing. Isabel loved to dance.

"You ought to look a little more peppy[16]," Valerie said one day in the women's room of the office. "You look too serious sometimes, Isabel. Scares men off, you know?"

Prissy had been present, doing her lips[17] in the mirror, and they had all laughed a little, even Isabel. Isabel took that remark, as she had taken others, seriously. She would try to look more lighthearted, like Valerie. Once the girls had remarked on a blouse Isabel had been wearing. This had been just after her mother's death. The blouse had been lavender and white with ruffles[18] around the neck and down the front like a jabot[19]. The girls had pronounced it "too old" for her, and maybe it had been, though Isabel had thought it **perky**. Anyway, Isabel had never worn it again. The girls meant well, Isabel knew, because they realized that she had spent the preceding five years in a sad way, nursing her mother practically single-handed. Isabel's father had died of a heart attack when Isabel had been nineteen, and fortunately he had left some life insurance, but that hadn't been enough for Isabel and her mother to engage a private nurse to come in now and then, even part-time.

---

14 accompanying
15 *old-fashioned, mainly literary*: a meeting, especially one that was not planned
16 *informal, US*: lively or full of energy
17 phrase *'doing her lips'*: putting on lipstick
18 a fold that decorates a piece of clothing
19 *unusual*: an ornamental ruffle on the front of a shirt or blouse

Isabel missed her father. He had been a tailor and presser[20] at a dry cleaning shop, and when Isabel's mother's illness had begun, her father had started working overtime, knowing that her cancer was going to be a long and expensive business. Isabel was sure that this was what had led to his heart attack. Her father, a short man with brown and grey hair and a modest manner that Isabel loved, had used to come home stooped[21] with **fatigue** around ten at night, but always able to swing his arms forward and give Isabel a smile and ask, "How's my favourite girl tonight?" Sometimes he put his hands lightly on her shoulders and kissed her cheek, sometimes not, as if he were even too tired for that, or as if he thought she might not like it.

As for social life, Isabel realized that she hadn't progressed much since she had been seventeen and eighteen, dating now and then with boys she had met through her high-school acquaintances, and her high school had been an all-girls school. Isabel considered herself not a knock-out[22], perhaps, but not bad looking either. She was five feet six inches with light brown hair that was inclined to wave, which made a short hair-do easy and soft looking. She had a clear skin, light brown eyes (though she wished her eyes were larger), good teeth, and a medium-sized nose which only slightly turned up. She had of course, checked herself as long as she could remember for the usual faults, body odour or bad breath, or hair on the legs. Very important, those little matters.

Shortly after Prissy's remark about her looking too serious, Isabel went to a party in Brooklyn given by one of her old high-school friends who was getting married, and Isabel tried deliberately to be merry and talkative. There had been a most attractive young man called Charles Gramm or maybe Graham, tall and fair-haired, with a friendly smile and a rather shy manner. Isabel chatted with him for several minutes, and would have been thrilled if he had asked when he might see her again,

20 someone who 'presses', or irons, clothes
21 *literary:* walking or standing with your head and shoulders bent forwards and downwards
22 *US, informal:* very attractive

but he hadn't. Later, Isabel reproached herself for not having invited Charles to a drinks party or a Sunday **brunch** at her apartment.

This she did a week or so later, inviting Harriet, her Brooklyn hostess, and her fiancé, and asking Harriet to invite Charles, since Harriet must know how to reach him. Harriet did, Charles promised to come, Harriet said, and then didn't or couldn't. Isabel's brunch went quite well with the office girls (all except one who couldn't make it), but Isabel had no male partner in her efforts, and the brunch did not net[23] her a boyfriend either.

Isabel read a great deal. She liked romance novels with happy endings. She had loved romances since she had been fourteen or so, and since her mother's death, when she had more time, she read three or four a week. Most of them borrowed from the Public Library, a few bought in paperback. She preferred reading romance novels to watching TV dramas in the evening. Whole novels with descriptions of landscapes and details of houses put her into another world. The romances were rather like a drug, she realized as she felt herself drawn in the evenings towards the living-room sofa where lay her latest treasures, yet as drugs went, books were harmless, Isabel thought. They certainly weren't pot[24] or cocaine, which Prissy said she indulged in at parties sometimes. Isabel loved the first meetings of girl and man in these novels, the magnetic attraction of each for each, the **hurdles** that had to be got over before they were united. The terrible handicaps made her tense in body and mind, yet in the end, all came out well.

One day in April, a tall and handsome young man with dark hair strode into the lobby of Weiler and Diggs, though Isabel was not at the reception desk that day. Valerie was. Isabel was just then carrying a stack of photostatted[25] papers weighing nearly ten pounds across the lobby to Mr Diggs's office, and she saw Valerie's mascaraed[26] lashes flutter, her smile widen as she looked up at the young man and said, "Good morning, sir. Can

---

23 to manage to obtain
24 *informal:* the drug cannibis
25 photocopied
26 *unusual:* painted with mascara, a dark substance used for making eyelashes look darker and/or longer

I help you?"

As it happened, the young man came into Mr Diggs's office a minute later, while Isabel was putting the photostats away. Then Mr Diggs said:

"... in another office. Isabel? Can you get Area six six A file for me? Isn't that in Current?"

"Yes, sir, and it's right here. One of these." Isabel pulled out the folder that Mr Diggs wanted from near the bottom of the stack she had just brought in.

"Good girl, thanks," said Mr Diggs.

Isabel started for the door, and the eyes for the door, and the eyes of the young man met hers for an instant, and Isabel felt a **pang** go through her. Did that mean something important? Isabel carefully opened the door, and closed it behind her.

In less than five minutes, Mr Diggs summoned her back. He wanted more photostats of two pages from the file. Isabel made the copies and brought them back. This time the young man did not glance at her, but Isabel was conscious of his broad shoulders under his neat dark blue jacket.

Isabel ate her coffee-shop lunch that day **in a daze**. Valerie and Linda (one of the not-so-pretty secretaries) were with her.

"Who was that Tarzan[27] that came in this morning?" Linda asked with a mischievous smile, as if she really didn't care. She had addressed Valerie.

"Oh, wasn't he ever[28]! He ought to be in movies instead of – whatever he's doing." Valerie giggled. "His name's Dudley Hall. Dudley. Imagine."

Dudley Hall. Suddenly the tall, dark man had an identity for Isabel. His name sounded like one of the characters in the novels she read. Isabel didn't say a word.

Around four that afternoon, Dudley Hall was back. Isabel didn't see him come in, but when she was summoned to Mr Diggs's office, there he was. Mr Diggs put her on to more details about the office space on Lexington Avenue that Mr Hall was

27 a fictional character raised in the jungle by apes, who grows into a strong, silent, heroic character
28 *colloquial, phrase 'wasn't he ever!'*: used for emphasising that someone has a particular quality

interested in. This job took nearly an hour. Mr Hall came with her into another office (used by the secretaries, empty now), and Isabel had to make four telephone calls on Mr Hall's behalf, which she did with courtesy and patience, writing down neatly the information she gleaned about conditions of floors and walls, and the time space could be seen, and who had the keys now. As Mr Hall pocketed her notes, he said, "That's very kind of you, Miss –"

"Isabel," she said with a smile. "Not kind. Just my job. Isabel Crane, my name is. If you need any extra information – quick service, just ask for Isabel."

He smiled back. "I'll do that. Could I phone my partner now?"

"Indeed, yes! Go ahead," said Isabel, indicating a telephone on the desk. "You can dial[29] direct on this one."

Isabel lingered, straightening papers on the desk, awaiting a possible question or a request from Mr Hall to note down something. But he was only making a date with his partner whom he called Al to meet him in half an hour at the Lexington address. Then Mr Hall left.

Had he noticed her at all? Isabel wondered. Or was she just another face among the dozen or so girl secretaries he had seen lately? Isabel could almost believe she was in love with him, but to be in love was dangerous as well as being pleasant: she might never see Dudley Hall again.

By the middle of the next week, the picture had changed. There were a few legal matters that caused Mr Hall to come to Weiler and Diggs several times. Isabel was called in each time, because by now she was familiar with the file. She typed letters, and provided Dudley Hall and Albert Frenay with clear, concise memos[30].

"I think I owe you a drink – or a meal," said Dudley Hall with his handsome smile. "Can't make it tonight, but how is tomorrow? There's The Brewery right downstairs. Good steaks

---

29 to press the buttons or turn the dial on a telephone in order to call someone
30 a short note that you send someone you work with

there, I've tried 'em. Want to make it around six or whenever you get off? Or is that too early?"

Isabel suggested half past six, if that was all right with him.

She felt in the clouds[31], really in another world, yet one in which she was a principal character. She didn't mention her date to Valerie or Prissy, both of whom had commented on her "devotion" to Dudley Hall in the last days. Isabel had made the date for 6.30 so she would have time to get home and change before appearing at The Brewery.

She did go home, and **fussed** so long over her makeup, that she had to take a taxi to The Brewery. She had rather expected to see Dudley Hall standing near the door inside, or maybe at the bar, but she didn't see him. At one of the tables? She looked around. No. After checking[32] her light coat, Isabel moved towards the bar, and obtained a seat only because a man got up and gave her his, saying he didn't mind standing up. He was talking to a friend on an adjacent stool. Isabel told the barman she was waiting for someone, and would be only a minute. She kept glancing at the door whenever it opened, which was every fifteen seconds. At twenty to seven, she ordered a scotch[33] and soda. Dudley was probably working a bit late or had had difficulty getting a taxi. He'd be full of apologies, which Isabel would say were quite unnecessary. She had tidied her apartment, and the coffee-maker was clean and ready, in case he would accept her invitation to come up for a final coffee at the end of the evening. She had brandy also, though she was not fond of it.

The music, gentle from the walls, was old Cole Porter[34] songs. The voices and laughter around her gave her cheer[35], and the aroma of freshly broiled[36] steaks began to make her hungry. The decor was old brown wood and polished brass, masculine but romantic, Isabel thought. She checked her appearance in the

---

31 *colloquial, phrase* 'in the clouds': to be thinking your own thoughts and not concentrating on what is happening around you; usually 'to have your head in the clouds'
32 *US*: to give your coat to the attendant of a cloakroom
33 whisky produced in Scotland
34 famous US composer and songwriter (died 1964)
35 *mainly literary*: a feeling of happiness
36 *US*: grilled or barbecued food

mirror above the row of closely set bottles. She was wearing her best 'little black frock'[37] with a V-neck, a slender gold chain that she had inherited from her mother, earrings of jade[38]. She had washed her hair early that morning, and she was looking her best. In a moment, she thought, glancing again at the door, Dudley would walk in hurriedly, looking around for her, **spotting** her and smiling when she raised her hand.

When Isabel next looked at her watch, she saw that it was a couple of minutes past 7.30. A painful shock went through her, making her almost **shudder**. Up to then, she had been able to believe he was just a little late, that a waiter would page[39] her, calling out "Miss *Crane*?", to tell her that Mr Hall would be arriving at any minute, but now Isabel realized that he might not be arriving. She was on her second scotch which she had been sipping slowly so it would last, and she still had half of it.

"Waiting for somebody? – Buy you a drink in the meantime?" asked a heavy-set man on her left, the opposite side from the door side, whom Isabel had noticed observing her for several minutes.

"No, thanks," Isabel said with a quick smile, and looked away from him. She knew his type, just another lone wolf[40] looking for a pick-up and maybe an easy, unimportant roll in the hay[41] later. Hello and goodbye. Not her dish at all.

At about five minutes to eight, Isabel paid for her drinks and departed. She thought she had waited long enough. Either Dudley Hall didn't want to see her, or he had had a **mishap**. Isabel imagined a broken leg from a fall down some stairs, a **mugging** on the street which had left him unconscious. She knew these possibilities were most unlikely.

The next day Dudley Hall did telephone to make his excuses. He had been **stuck** at a meeting with his partner plus two other colleagues from six o'clock until nearly eight, he said, and it had

---

37 *old-fashioned: dress;* 'little black frock/dress' *is one worn on formal occasions*
38 a hard green substance used for making jewellery
39 *US:* to call someone's name in a public place (or to leave a message on a small machine called a pager which they carry with them)
40 someone who likes to be, or work, alone
41 *colloquial, phrase* 'roll in the hay': having spontaneous, uncommitted sex

been impossible to get away for two minutes to make a phone call, and he was terribly sorry.

"Oh – not so important. I understand," said Isabel pleasantly. She had rehearsed her words, in case he telephoned.

"I thought by seven-thirty or so you'd surely have left, so I didn't try to call The Brewery."

"Yes, I had left. Don't worry about it."

"Well – another time, maybe. Sorry about last night, Isabel."

They hung up, leaving Isabel with a sense of shock, not knowing how the last few seconds had passed, causing them both to hang up so quickly.

The following Sunday morning, Isabel went to the Metropolitan Museum to **browse** for an hour or so, then she took a leisurely stroll in Central Park. It was a sunny spring morning. People were airing[42] their dogs, and mothers and nurses – women in uniforms, nannies of wealthy families – pushed baby carriages or sat on benches chatting, with the carriages turned so the babies would get the most sun. Isabel's eyes drifted often from the trees, which she loved to gaze at, to the babies and toddlers learning to walk, their hands held by their fathers and mothers.

It had occurred to her that Dudley Hall was not going to call her again. She could telephone him easily, and invite him for a Sunday brunch or simply for a drink at her apartment. But she was afraid that might look too forward, as if she were trying too hard.

Dudley Hall did not come again to the office, because he had no need to, Isabel realized. Nevertheless, meeting him had been exciting, she couldn't deny that. Those few hours when she had thought she had a date with him – well, she'd *had* one – had been more than happy, she'd been ecstatic as she'd never been in her life that she could remember. She had felt a little the way she did when reading a good romance novel, but her date had been real. Dudley had meant to keep it, she was sure. He could have done better about phoning, but Isabel believed that he had been **tied up**.

---

42 taking outside for fresh, warm air

The Romantic

In her evenings alone, doing some chore like washing drip-dry blouses and hanging them on the rack over the tub, Isabel relived those minutes in The Brewery, when she had been looking so well, and had been expecting Dudley to walk through the door at any second. That had been enchantment. Black magic. If she concentrated, or sometimes if she didn't, a thrill went over her as she imagined his tall figure, his eyes finding her after he came through the big brown door of The Brewery.

Eva Rosenau, a good friend of her mother's, called her up one evening and insisted on **popping over**, as she had just made a sauerbraten[43] and wanted to give Isabel some. Isabel could hardly decline, as Eva lived nearby and could walk to Isabel's building, and besides, Eva had been so helpful with her mother, Isabel felt rather in her debt. Eva arrived, bearing a heavy iron casserole. "I know you always loved sauerbraten, Isabel. Are you eating enough, my child? You look a little pale."

"Really? – I don't feel pale." Isabel smiled. The sauerbraten was still a bit warm and gave off a delicious smell of ginger gravy and well-cooked beef. "This does look divine, Eva," said Isabel, meaning it.

They put the meat and gravy into another pot so Eva could take her casserole home. Isabel washed the big pot at the sink. Then she offered Eva a glass of wine, which Eva always enjoyed.

Eva was about sixty and had three grown children, none of whom lived with her. She had never had a job, but she could do a lot of things – fix faulty plumbing, knit, make electrical repairs, and she even knew something about nursing and could give injections. She was also motherly, or so Isabel had always felt. She had dark curly hair, now half grey, was a bit **stocky**, and dressed as if she didn't care how she looked as long as she was covered. Now she complimented Isabel on how neat the apartment looked.

"Bet you're glad to see the last of those bedpans[44]!" Eva said, laughing.

---

43 a German dish cooked in the oven
44 a wide flat container used as a toilet by people who are too ill to get out of bed

Isabel rolled her eyes upwards and tried to smile, not wanting to think about bedpans. She had **chucked** the two of them long ago.

"Are you going out enough?" asked Eva, in an armchair now with her glass of wine. "Not too lonely?"

Isabel assured her that she wasn't.

"Theo's coming for Sunday dinner, bringing a man friend from his office. Come have dinner with us, Isabel! Around one. Not sauerbraten. Something different. Do you good, dear, and it's just two steps from here."

Theo was one of Eva's sons. "I'll – That's nice of you, Eva."

"*Nice?*" Eva frowned. "We'll expect you," she said firmly.

Isabel didn't go. She got up the courage to call Eva around ten on Sunday morning and to tell a small lie, which she disliked doing. She said she had extra work for the office to do at home, and though it wasn't a lot of work, she thought she should not interrupt it by going out at midday. It would have been easier to say she wasn't feeling well or had a cold, but in that case, Eva would have been over with some kind of medicine or hot soup.

Sunday afternoon Isabel **tackled** the apartment with a new, calmer determination. There were more of her mother's **odds and ends** to throw away, little things like old scarves that Isabel knew she would never wear. She moved the sofa to the other side of the room, nearer a front window, and put a settle between window and sofa to serve as an end table, a much better role for that object, and Isabel was sorry she hadn't thought of it before. "Settle" was not even the right word for these chair-tables, Isabel had found by accident when looking into the dictionary for something else. A settle had a back to it and was longer. Another, one of many, odd usage of her mother's. The sofa rearrangement caused a change in the position of the coffee table and an armchair, transforming the living room, making it look bigger and more cheerful. Isabel realized that she was lucky with her three-room apartment. It was in an old building, and the rent had gone up only slightly in the fifteen years since her family had had it. She could hardly have found a one-room-and-kitchenette these days for the rent she was paying now. Isabel was happy also because she had a plan for that Sunday evening.

Her plan, her intention, kept her in a good mood all the afternoon, even though she deliberately did not think hard about it. *Play it cool*, she told herself. Around five, she put a favourite Sinatra[45] cassette on, and danced by herself.

By seven, she was in a large but rather cosy bar on Sixth Avenue in the upper 50s. Again she wore her pretty black dress with the V-neck, a jade or at least green-bead necklace, and no earrings. She pretended she had a date around 7.30, not with Dudley Hall necessarily, but with somebody. Again she sat at the bar and ordered a scotch and soda, sipped it slowly while she cast, from time to time, a glance at the door. And she looked at her watch calmly every once in a while. She knew no one was going to walk in who had a date with her, but she could look around at the mostly **jolly** crowd with a different feeling now, quite without anxiety, as if she were one of them. She could even chat with the businessman-type on the stool next to hers (though she didn't accept his invitation to have a drink on him), saying to him that she was waiting for someone. She did not feel in the least **awkward** or alone, as she had finally felt at The Brewery. During her second drink, she imagined her date: a blond man this time, around thirty-four, tall and athletic with a face just slightly **creased** from the cold winds he had braved when skiing. He'd have large hands and be rather the Scandinavian type. She looked for such a man when she next lifted her head and sought the faces of three or four men who were coming in the door. Isabel was aware that a couple of people around her had noticed, without interest, that she was awaiting someone. This made her feel infinitely more at ease than if she had been at the bar all by herself, as it were.

At a quarter to eight, she departed cheerfully, yet with an air of slight impatience which she affected for any observer, as if she had given up hope that the person she was waiting for would arrive.

---

45 US singer, popular all over the world (died 1998)

Once at home, she put on more comfortable clothes and switched on the TV for a few minutes, feeling relaxed and happy, as if she'd had a pleasant drinks hour out somewhere. She prepared some dinner for herself, then mended a loose hook[46] at the waist of one of her skirts, and then it was still early enough to read a few pages in her current romance novel, *A Caged Heart*, before she went to bed, taking the book with her.

Valerie remarked that she was looking happier. Isabel hadn't realized this, but she was glad to hear it. She was happier lately. Now she was going out – dressing up nicely of course – twice a week on her fantasy dates, as she liked to think of them. What was the **harm**? And she never ordered more than two drinks, so it was even an inexpensive way of entertaining herself, never more than six or seven dollars an evening. She had a **hazy** collection of men with whom she had had imaginary dates in the past weeks, as hazy as the faces of girls she had known in high-school, whose faces she was beginning to have trouble identifying when she looked into her graduation book[47], because most of the girls had been only a part of the coming and going and dropping-out[48] landscape of the overcrowded school. The Scandinavian type and a dark man a bit like Dudley Hall did stand out to Isabel, because she had imagined that they had gone on from drinks to dinner, and then perhaps she had asked them back to her apartment. There could be a second date with the same man, of course. Isabel never imagined them in bed with her, though the men might have proposed this.

Isabel invited Eva Rosenau one Saturday for lunch, and served cold ham and potato salad and a good chilled white wine. Eva was pleased, appreciative, and she said she was glad Isabel was **perking up**, by which Isabel knew she meant that she no longer looked under the shadow of her mother's death. Isabel had finally thrown out the old curtains, not even wanting to use them for **rags** lest

---

46 a curved piece of metal or plastic for hanging things on
47 *US*: a book students get when they leave high school, containing photographs of fellow students, amongst other things
48 *colloquial*: leaving something such as school or an activity before you have finished what you intended to do

The Romantic | 131

she be reminded of drearier days, and she had **run up** new light green curtains on her mother's sewing machine.

"Good huntin'!" Valerie said to Isabel, Valerie was off on her vacation. "Maybe you've got a secret heart interest now. Have you?"

Isabel was staying on at the office, taking her vacation last. "Is that all you think makes the world go round?" Isabel replied, but she felt the colour rise to her cheeks as if she had a secret boyfriend whose identity she would spring on the girls when she invited them to her engagement party. "You and Roger have a ball!" Valerie was going off with her steady boyfriend with whom she was now living.

Four days before Isabel was to get her two weeks' vacation, she was called to the telephone by Prissy who was at the reception desk. Isabel took it in another office.

"Willy," the voice said. "Remember me? Wilbur Miller from Nebraska?" He laughed.

Isabel suddenly remembered a man of about thirty, not very tall, not very handsome, who had come to the office a few days ago and had found some office space. She remembered that he had said, when he had given his name for her to write down, "Really Wilbur. Nobody's named Wilbur any more and nobody comes from Nebraska, but I do." Isabel said finally into the telephone, "Yes."

"Well – got any objections if I ask you out for dinner? Say Friday night? Just to say thanks, you know – Isabel."

"N-no. That's very nice of you, Mr Miller."

"Willy. I was thinking of a restaurant downtown. Greenwich Street. It's called the Imperial Fish. You like fish? Lobster?" Before she could answer, he went on. Should he pick her up at the office Friday, or would she prefer to meet him at the restaurant?

"I can meet you – where you said, if you give me the address."

He had the address for her. They agreed upon seven.

Isabel looked at the address and telephone number of the Imperial Fish, which she had written down. Now she remembered Wilbur Miller very well. He had an openness and informality that was unlike most New Yorkers, she recalled, and at the same time he had looked full of self-confidence. He had wanted a two-room office, something to do with distribution of parts. Electronic parts? That didn't matter. She also remembered that she had felt an unusual **awareness** of him, something like friendliness and excitement at the same time. Funny. But she hadn't **put herself out for him**. She had smothered[49] her feelings and even affected a little formality. Could Willy Miller of Nebraska be Mister Right? The knight on a white horse[50], as they said jokingly in some of the romances she read, with whom she was destined to spend the rest of her life?

Between then and Friday evening, Isabel's mind or memory **shied away from** what Willy Miller looked like, what his voice was like, though she well remembered. She was aware that her knees trembled, maybe her hands also, a couple of times on Friday.

Friday around six, Isabel dressed for her date with Willy Miller. She was not taking so much trouble with her appearance as she had for Dudley Hall, she thought, and it was true. A sleeveless dress of pale blue, because it was a warm evening, a raincoat of nearly transparent plastic, since rain was forecast, nice white sandals, and that was it.

She was in front of the Imperial Fish's blue-and-white striped awning[51] at five past seven, and she glanced around for Willy among the people on the sidewalk[52], but he was probably in the restaurant, waiting for her. Isabel walked several paces in the uptown direction, then turned and strolled back, under the awning and past it. She wondered why she was hesitating. To make herself more interesting by being late? No. This evening with Willy could be just a nice evening, with dinner and

---

49 *unusual, literary:* to try not to express a feeling
50 *romantic, phrase 'knight on a white horse':* a man who helps someone, especially a woman, who is sad or in trouble
51 a sheet of cloth hung above a window or door as protection against rain or sun, especially outside a shop
52 *American:* pavement

conversation, and maybe coffee back at her apartment, maybe not.

What if she stood him up? She looked again at the awning and repressed a nervous laugh. He'd order a second drink, and keep glancing at the door, as she always did. He'd learn to know what it felt like. However, she had nothing whatsoever against Willy Miller. She simply realized that she didn't want to spend the evening with him, didn't want to make better acquaintance with him. She sensed that she could start an affair with him, which because she was older and wiser would be more important than the silly experience – She didn't know what to call that one-night affair with the second of her loves, who hadn't been even as important as the first, with whom she'd never been to bed. The second had been the married man.

She wanted to go back home. Or did she? Frowning, she stared at the door of the Imperial Fish. Should she go in and say, "Hello, Willy. Sorry I'm late"? Or "I'm sorry, Willy, but I don't want to keep this date."

I prefer my own dates, she might add. That was the truth.

A passerby **bumped** her shoulder, because she was standing still in the middle of the sidewalk. She set her teeth. *I'm going home*, she told herself, like a command, and she began to walk uptown in the direction of where she lived, and because she was in rather good clothes, she treated herself to a taxi.

Post-reading exercises

Understanding the story

1 **Use these questions to check that you have understood the story.**

Isabel's history

1 How old is Isabel? Why didn't she go to college?
2 When did Isabel's mother die?
3 What has Isabel's social life been like so far?
4 What does Isabel hope for after her mother's death? Does this happen?
5 What is Isabel's job? What opportunities does she have at work to meet men?
6 What happened to Isabel's father? How did this affect Isabel's life?
7 What happened at the party in Brooklyn?
8 Who did Isabel invite to her house? Did everybody come?

Isabel's life

9 What kind of books does Isabel like to read?
10 Who is Dudley Hall? What does Isabel think of him?
11 Where does Dudley invite Isabel? What time do they arrange to meet?
12 What happens at the bar? How long does Isabel wait?
13 Why does Dudley phone the next day?
14 Who is Eva Rosenau? Why does she visit Isabel?
15 What excuse does Isabel make for not going to Eva's house?
16 What does Isabel do on Sunday afternoon? And in the evening?
17 How often does Isabel go out on her 'dates'? How do they make her feel?
18 Who is Wilbur Miller and why does he phone Isabel?
19 Does Isabel keep her date with Wilbur Miller?
20 How does Isabel explain her own behaviour to herself?

Language study

Grammar

Discourse markers

Discourse markers are words and phrases which link up longer sections of text. Sometimes, they show the connection between what has been said and what is coming next (e.g. *anyway*); sometimes they show someone's attitude (e.g. *frankly*); sometimes, they show what kind of communication is going on (e.g. the use of *after all* in persuading).

Look at these examples of discourse markers from the story:

Introducing a contrast with what has gone before
Yet *six weeks after her mother's funeral, Isabel found that her life had not changed much after all.*
However, *she had nothing whatsoever against Willy Miller.*

Showing someone's attitude to something
Isabel had ... a job, **of course**, *to help with finances.*

Dismissing what has gone before
Anyway, *Isabel had never worn it again.*

Focusing on a topic
As for *social life, Isabel realised that she hadn't progressed much.*

Referring to someone's expectations
As it happened, *the young man came into Mr. Digg's office a minute later.*

Introducing a stronger argument than the one before
Isabel could hardly decline, as Eva lived nearby ... and **besides**, *Eva had been so helpful with her mother.*

Making a statement sound less definite
This made her feel infinitely more at ease than if she had been at the bar all by herself, **as it were**.

1 Use the examples above to help you to complete the sentences below with a suitable discourse marker.

1 I was going to phone him and ask him out but, ..., he turned up at my house that same evening.
2 I don't know what time I'll arrive; perhaps eight o'clock or quarter past. .... I'll definitely be there before half past.
3 He was quiet and ordinary-looking and .... there was something very attractive about him.

136 | *The Romantic*

4 You've all behaved disgracefully, and as .... you, young man, you can forget all about going to the concert!
5 You could say that he did not behave very well towards women in his youth; he 'spread his affections around' ....
6 I'm not sure that she deserves an increase in salary. She hasn't worked very hard and her attitude is very negative. ...., she received a huge bonus only six months ago!
7 The council accepts full responsibility for the accident and will, ..., award full compensation to the victims.
8 I don't really want to go to the party. ...., Freda will be very disappointed if I don't, so I'll make the effort.

Vocabulary

Formal and informal vocabulary

A peculiarity of Highsmith's style is the way she combines informal and formal vocabulary. It is hard to know how far this is deliberate on her part, but it adds to the disturbing effect of her narrative.

Notice how strange it seems to include the informal verb *chuck* in the middle of this otherwise formal sentence:

> *Then there were the old books, not even classics, which filled more than half of the two bookcases (otherwise filled with better books or at least newer books), which Isabel imagined chucking, thereby leaving space for the occasional objet d'art or statuette or something, such as she had seen in magazine photographs of attractive living-room interiors.* [page 119]

2 Which of these pairs of words is more formal?

1 Most young people *started/embarked on* a college course at 18.
2 Those new tables with five legs are a bit *eccentric/nutty*, aren't they?
3 I'm going to spend tomorrow *throwing out/chucking out* all my old clothes.
4 Don sold his old bicycle, *thereby/so* creating more space in the garage.
5 It is part of my job to *escort/go with* clients to the head office.
6 Isabel did not consider herself to be a *knock-out/beauty*.
7 Isabel checked herself for things like body odour and *halitosis/bad breath*.
8 In five minutes, the boss *called/summoned* Isabel back to the office.
9 Isabel believed that Dudley had really been *occupied/tied up* at the meeting.

10 Eva arrived *bearing/carrying* a heavy casserole.

The use of *rather*

The word *rather* is an adverb of degree and is used to modify adjectives and certain expressions. In the story, it tends to give an effect of vagueness or understatement. Isabel's external reactions are never extreme or violent. The use of *rather* underlines the apparent normality of her perceptions and attitudes.

It is usually used as *rather* + verb or *rather* + adjective in 'positive' terms, to say what someone or something *is* or *has*, e.g. *he is rather nice, that table is rather large*. Be careful to use it with adjectives that can be modified; it should *not* be used with absolutes, for example, *the possibilities are rather infinite*.

Look at these examples from the story:

> *They* [the settles] *looked fragile,* **rather** *like little tables.*
> *… with a friendly smile and a* **rather** *shy manner.*
> *The romances were* **rather** *like a drug, she realized.*
> *Isabel felt* **rather** *in her debt.*
> *… because she was in* **rather** *good clothes, she treated herself to a taxi.*

3 Which of these sentences are incorrect?
1 I rather enjoy being by myself.
2 He was rather handsome, with dark hair and brown eyes.
3 I don't think that's rather a good idea.
4 Don't you think the car's rather expensive?
5 She's rather like her mother but a lot taller.
6 I feel rather bad about standing him up.
7 The job you are asking me to do is rather impossible.
8 That combination of blue and cream is rather perfect.

Clichés

A cliché is an overused phrase or opinion. In the story, Isabel sometimes thinks in terms of clichés which are associated with romance or romantic novels. For example, she says, *"Is that all you think makes the world go round?"*, after Valerie teases her about having a secret boyfriend. This is a reference to the expression 'love makes the world go round'. What does this phrase mean?

4 What is the meaning of these clichés from the story?

1 *She felt in the clouds*
2 *Mister Right*
3 *The knight on a white horse*

5 Now look at these clichés. What do you think they mean?

1 Life is not a bed of roses.
2 You can't have it all.
3 Reach for the stars.
4 It's not the end of the world.
5 Time is a great healer.
6 My better half.
7 There's no place like home.
8 There's no time like the present.

Literary analysis

Plot

1 Write these events from the story in the correct order:
   a Isabel goes on her first fantasy date.
   b Isabel's father dies.
   c Isabel meets Dudley Hall at work.
   d Eva invites Isabel to Sunday dinner.
   e Isabel leaves school.
   f Wilbur Miller invites Isabel to go out to dinner.
   g Isabel's mother dies.
   h Isabel invites Harriet and some other people to her house.
   i Dudley Hall does not keep his date with Isabel.
2 Which of the above events affect Isabel most? Which event leads her to start her fantasy dates?
3 Are there many causes for Isabel's fantasy dates or just one?
4 Why do you think Highsmith describes Isabel's flat in such detail?
5 Are Isabel's fantasy dates harmless? Why/why not?
6 Would you describe *The Romantic* as a love story? If not, what kind of story is it?
7 Does the story seem old-fashioned to you or do you think it could happen today?

Character

8 Which of these adjectives describe Isabel?

| beautiful | imaginative | hard-working | optimistic | polite |
| damaged | lonely | unlucky | afraid | brave | cynical |

Can you think of two other adjectives to describe her?
9 How does Isabel see herself? How do the other women in the office see her?
10 What is your impression of Dudley Hall? And Wilbur Miller? Why does Isabel not keep her date with Wilbur?
11 Highsmith writes: *Isabel missed her father.* What is your impression of Isabel's relationship with her parents? Do you think she misses her mother?
12 Which people in the story do you think are most sympathetic towards Isabel? Who do you think would be most understanding if they knew the truth about her fantasy dates?
13 How does Highsmith portray Isabel as an ordinary young woman? How does she differ from the other women in the office?
14 What do you think Highsmith is saying in the story about human behaviour?

Narration

15 Highsmith's narrative voice is sometimes described as 'deceptively normal'. What details does she give which reinforce the impression of normality? Think about the description of rooms, furniture, clothes, food, work etc.
16 What are the moments of drama in the story? Are they told through dialogue or description? What effect does this have?
17 Highsmith does not explain people's motives. Why do you think this is? Think about why Isabel does not go to Eva's house for dinner, and why she does not keep her date with Wilbur.
18 Look again at the passage where Isabel goes for a walk in the park. What details does Highsmith describe? What is the effect?
19 Highsmith often narrates important events or feelings in short sentences e.g. *Isabel missed her father, Isabel read a great deal, Isabel didn't go.* Find some more examples. What do they describe? What effect do they have?

Atmosphere

20 The writer Graham Greene commented that every time he read Patricia Highsmith's fiction, he felt 'a sense of personal danger.' Could his description apply to *The Romantic*? Think about how Highsmith makes the reader sympathise and identify with Isabel.
21 Make a list of the different locations in the story: Isabel's flat, her workplace, the bars. What is the atmosphere like in each place? Think about furniture, music, people, activities etc.
22 Think about Isabel's inner dialogue. How is it different to what she says to other people? What effect does this create?
23 Which of these adjectives describe the atmosphere of the story? Can you think of any more?

unrealistic	disturbing	amusing	reassuring	sinister
worrying				

Style

24 One feature of Highsmith's style is to include details which 'jar' or are surprising in some way (see the example in the Vocabulary section on 'Formal and informal language', page 137). This has the effect of reminding us that things are not as normal or comfortable as they first seem.
   a) Look at the first conversation between Isabel and Eva [page 128-9]. Which word shows that Eva is a little surprised or worried about Isabel?
   b) Look at the passage [page 129] where Isabel moves the furniture around in her flat. Which sentence suggests that Isabel's relationship with her mother was difficult?
25 Much of the narrative describes Isabel's thought processes. Find a passage where Highsmith describes what Isabel is thinking, for example, when she is waiting for Dudley in the bar, or when she is trying to remember Wilbur Miller.
   a) How does Highsmith make Isabel's inner monologue convincing?
   b) Think about how Isabel censors her own thoughts, criticises herself, and how she mixes everyday detail and imagination.

26 Find some examples of humour in the story, for example when Eva discusses the bedpans with Isabel. For example, think about Eva's reference to bedpans and Isabel's concern with personal hygiene. Is it fair to say that Highsmith's humour is 'dark'?
27 Highsmith rarely describes suffering or trauma in a direct way. When does she break this rule? What language does she use? What effect does this have?

Guidance to the above literary terms, answer keys to all the exercises and activities, plus a wealth of other reading-practice material, can be found on the student's section of the Macmillan Readers website at: www.macmillanenglish.com/readers.

Full Circle
by Edith Wharton

About the author

Edith Wharton was a famous US novelist, short-story writer and designer. She was a member of an aristocratic New York family and knew many of the leading literary and public figures of her time. Her best-known novel, *The Age of Innocence*, won the 1921 Pulitzer Prize[1] and was made into an award-winning film starring Winona Ryder and Daniel Day Lewis.

Edith Newbold Jones was born in 1862 in New York City to a wealthy family. She had two older brothers who were 12 and 16 years older than her. When she was four years old her family set off to travel around Europe, visiting Italy, Spain, Germany and France. After five years of travelling they returned to New York and Edith was educated at home by private tutors. She was interested in literature and telling stories from a young age, even though her family did not encourage her interests.

At the age of 23 she married a wealthy banker, Teddy Wharton, who was 12 years older than her. He came from a wealthy Boston family and shared Edith's love of travel. However, they had little else in common and the marriage was not a happy one. Both Edith and her husband had affairs and the marriage eventually ended in divorce.

Edith published her first short story ('Mrs Mainstay's View') in 1899, at the age of 29. In the same year she also published her first collection of short stories, *The Greater Inclination*, and shortly afterwards, in 1902, her first novel, *The Valley of Decision*. She went on to write more than 60 books, including novels, short-story collections, essays, travel books and anthologies of poetry. In 1921 she became the first woman ever to win a Pulitzer prize.

Edith was also interested in design and architecture and her first book was not, in fact, a work of literature, but a book about interior design, *The Decoration of Houses*, which she wrote with the well-known

1 a prestigious US award. Pulitzer prizes are awarded every year in 21 categories covering newspaper journalism, literature and musical composition. It is regarded as the highest national honour in these fields.

architect, Ogden Codman, in 1897. The book was very popular and influential. Her home, The Mount, in Lenox, Massachusetts became a living example of her ideas, and it was opened to the public after her death. Edith wrote several of her novels here and often invited important literary figures to visit The Mount, including her good friend, Henry James. Edith and her husband lived there until 1911 when they moved to France. Their marriage deteriorated and in 1913 they got divorced. Edith sold The Mount and moved permanently to Paris.

When World War I broke out, Edith became active in helping refugees and orphans in France and Belgium. She helped women find jobs to support their families while the men were at war. She raised funds to set up and run hostels and schools. She toured battlefields and hospitals on the frontline and wrote about her experiences in two books, *Fighting France* (1915) and *The Marne* (1918). She was awarded the title of *Chevalier* (Knight) in the French Legion of Honour in 1916 for her work during the war.

At the end of the war she left her home in the centre of Paris and bought a house in the country nearby, at Pavillon Colombe in Saint-Brice-sous-Forêt. She lived there until her death in 1937. She is buried in the American Cemetery in Versailles. She continued to write up until her death and left an unfinished novel, *The Buccaneers*, which was published in its unfinished form in 1938. The novel was later completed by another US writer, Marion Mainwaring, using notes and a synopsis that Edith had written before her death. It was published in 1993.

About the story

'Full Circle' was published in October 1909. It first appeared in *Scribner's Magazine* and subsequently in *The Collected Short Stories of Edith Wharton*, published in the same year.

The title, 'Full Circle', comes from the idiomatic expression *to come full circle* used to describe a situation that becomes the same again as it was at the beginning.

Background information

Upper classes in New York

Much of Edith Wharton's writing is concerned with the upper classes in the USA at the end of the 19th century and the beginning of the 20th century. This was the world she grew up in and one she knew very well. Geoffrey Betton, the main character in 'Full Circle', is a member of the upper class. He lives on his own in a luxurious apartment in downtown New York City. He has a *valet* (a man servant) who looks after him. He *dresses for dinner* (changes into formal clothes when he is eating in the evening) even when he is eating at home. He employs a personal secretary to look after his mail.

Fifth Avenue

Geoffrey Betton lives on Fifth Avenue, a street in the centre of downtown New York City. Much of the street looks out over the city's Central Park. Fifth Avenue is a symbol of wealth in New York. It is still one of the most expensive streets in the world and one of the most exclusive shopping areas.

The Dead Letter Office

First opened in 1825, the Dead Letter Office is part of the United States postal service. It deals with mail that cannot be delivered to the address on the letter or parcel, for whatever reason. Where possible they try to find the recipient or someone who can accept the mail on their behalf. If the mail cannot be delivered, it is returned to the sender at no extra cost. If it cannot be returned to the sender, its contents are either destroyed or sold at auction.

Diadems and Faggots

Geoffrey Betton's first novel is *Diadems and Faggots*. A diadem is a type of crown and it is sometimes used as a symbol of power or dignity. A faggot is a bundle of firewood, and can symbolise humility or poverty.

Summary

It may help you to know something about what happens in the story before you read it. Don't worry, this summary does *not* tell you how the story ends.

Geoffrey Betton is a wealthy novelist. His first novel, *Diadems and Faggots*, was a great success. He lives in a flat on Fifth Avenue and is looked after by his valet. When he publishes his second novel, he decides to employ a secretary to read and answer all the fan letters he is expecting to receive.

An old friend of Betton's, Duncan Vyse, applies for the job. Betton still feels guilty about having let his friend down when they were both young and starting out on their careers, and he is happy to offer him the job. To start with everything goes well. Vyse deals efficiently with the large number of fan letters that start to appear days after Betton's second novel comes out. And Betton enjoys the novelty of having a secretary to read and answer all his letters.

However, after a few weeks, the letters start to get fewer and fewer. Betton suspects that Vyse is not showing him all the letters, but the truth is that his second novel is not as successful as his first. Betton feels embarrassed by the failure of his novel, and especially by the fact that Vyse is a witness to that failure. He feels uncomfortable and starts to thinks it is time to let his secretary go. He invites Vyse to dinner to break the news, but Vyse obviously needs the money and Betton can't bring himself to fire his friend.

Then more letters start to arrive, and the tone is different this time. It seems that new readers have found and loved the book. Vyse is busy and Betton is happy. There are two letter writers in particular that write again and again and Betton decides to get personally involved in the correspondence. But things get complicated when one of his replies is returned unopened.

Pre-reading exercises
Key vocabulary

This section will help you familiarise yourself with some of the more specific vocabulary used in the story. You may want to use it to help you before you start reading, or as a revision exercise after you have finished the story.

The story is set in the world of the New York City upper classes at the beginning of the 20th century. This is reflected in the vocabulary and language of the story.

Geoffrey Betton's apartment
1 Look at the words in bold and match them to their definitions.

Geoffrey Betton lives in an **apartment** on Fifth Avenue. He has a **valet** who looks after him. The valet comes into his bedroom every morning, opens the curtains and fills his **porcelain** bath in the **dressing-room** next to his bedroom. He places a crystal and silver **cigarette-box** at the side of his bed, lights a fire and opens the windows. All of this he does before Betton is awake. When Betton has had his bath, Strett, the valet, brings him his **breakfast tray** to his bedroom. On the tray is his **correspondence**. Once he has eaten Betton goes for a ride in the park and comes back in time for **luncheon**.

1 (mainly US English) a set of rooms for living in, usually on one floor of a large building; the usual British English word is **flat**
2 a flat piece of wood used to carry food, in this case the first meal of the day
3 an ornate container for cigarettes
4 a small room next to a bedroom where clothes are kept
5 (formal) a meal eaten at midday
6 a man whose job is to look after another man's clothes and cook his meals
7 a hard, shiny, white substance used for making expensive dishes, cups, decorations etc
8 mail or letters

What do they tell us about the main character Geoffrey Betton's lifestyle and home?

Upper-class speech

Both of the main characters, Geoffrey Betton and his secretary, Duncan Vyse, were educated at Harvard, one of the most prestigious universities in the USA, and their speech is often formal and contains vocabulary that is typical of the upper classes of the time.

2 Look at the examples below. Match the expressions from the story (1–10) to the expressions (a–j) we would use in modern speech.

1 Glad you looked me up, **my dear fellow**
2 A **chap** who carries deadly secrets
3 It's mostly awful **bosh**, you know
4 What **the deuce** could have become of it?
5 It will be **awfully jolly** finding out.
6 **By George – by George!** Won't she see it?
7 Not even the worst **twaddle** about my book?
8 Oh, I'm all right now – getting on **capitally**
9 **Poor devil**, I'm damned if I don't do it for him!
10 Why **the devil** don't he say out what he thinks?

a) I'm fine now, getting on really well
b) What can possibly have happened to it?
c) A man who has something to hide
d) I'm glad you came to see me
e) It'll be fun to find out
f) Most of it is complete nonsense
g) Wow! Won't she notice?
h) Why doesn't he just say what he thinks?
i) Not even the worst rubbish about my book?
j) Poor man, I'm going to help him out!

3 All the words in bold in the expressions 1–10 are old-fashioned and associated with the upper classes. Match them to their uses and meanings below.

a) used in questions for emphasising how surprised or annoyed you are
b) used for talking to a man in a friendly way
c) used to express enthusiasm
d) another word to express enthusiasm
e) used to express surprise
f) used for asking something in an angry way
g) another word to mean man

h) used to describe silly talk or writing
i) used to describe an unlucky man
j) another word to describe nonsense or silly talk

Feelings and attitudes

The author often uses formal vocabulary to talk about feelings and attitudes. Look at the words and their definitions. Which are positive, which are negative and which are neutral?

> **composure** the feeling of being calm, confident and relaxed
> **compunction** a feeling that you shouldn't do something because it is wrong
> **conduct** behaviour
> **delicacy** a sensitive and careful way of dealing with a difficult situation
> **derision** the opinion that someone or something is stupid, unimportant or useless
> **hauteur** proud and unfriendly behaviour
> **indolence** laziness
> **joy** a feeling of great happiness
> **magnanimity** a feeling of wanting to forgive people, to be kind and fair
> **rancour** a feeling of hate or anger that lasts a long time
> **truculence** being easily annoyed and ready to argue or fight
> **yearnings** a strong feeling of wanting something very much, especially something you may not be able to have

4 Use some of the formal words above to complete the sentences below.

1 Human .... is generally based on valid motives.
2 He had secret .... to become a famous writer.
3 He still felt a certain .... towards the man because he felt he had been treated badly in the past.
4 With a great gesture of ...., he decided to forgive him all his past crimes.
5 He could still remember the sense of .... and comfort his new home gave him when he first moved in.
6 Vyse always seemed calm and collected, but his .... made Betton suspect he might be hiding a dark secret.

Main themes

Before you read the story, you may want to think about some of the main themes that come up. The questions will help you think about the story as you are reading it for the first time. There is more discussion of the main themes in the *Literary analysis* section after the story.

Fame and fortune

The story explores how fame and newfound wealth can affect a person and their relationships to others.

5 As you read the story, ask yourself:

a) What is Geoffrey Betton's attitude to his newfound wealth?
b) What does he enjoy most about being rich and famous?
c) Does it affect the way he treats the people around him?
d) Does it affect the way people treat him?

Deceit and self-deceit

The story contains a number of examples of both deceit (dishonest behaviour that is intended to trick someone) and self-deceit (when you are dishonest with yourself).

6 As you read the story, ask yourself:

a) Who is deceiving who?
b) Why?
c) What is the effect of the deceit?

Self-esteem

Both of the main characters suffer from problems with their self-esteem (the feeling that you are as important as other people and that you deserve to be treated well).

7 As you read the story, ask yourself:

a) Which of the two main characters is the best writer?
b) Which of the characters has more confidence in his abilities?
c) Who is most influenced by the opinion of others?

★ ★ ★ ★

Full Circle

by Edith Wharton

Geoffrey Betton woke rather late – so late that the winter sunlight sliding across his warm red carpet struck his eyes as he turned on the pillow.

Strett, the valet, had been in, drawn the bath in the adjoining dressing-room, placed the crystal and silver cigarette-box at his side, put a match to the fire, and thrown open the windows to the bright morning air. It brought in, on the glitter of sun, all the shrill crisp morning noises – those piercing notes of the American thoroughfare[2] that seem to take a sharper vibration from the clearness of the medium through which they pass.

Betton raised himself languidly. That was the voice of Fifth Avenue below his windows. He remembered that when he moved into his rooms eighteen months before, the sound had been like music to him: the complex orchestration to which the tune of his new life was set. Now it filled him with horror and weariness, since it had become the symbol of the hurry and noise of that new life. He had been far less hurried in the old days when he had to be up by seven, and down at the office sharp at nine. Now that he got up when he chose, and his life had no fixed framework of duties, the hours hunted him like a pack of blood-hounds.

He dropped back on his pillows with a groan. Yes – not a year ago there had been a positively sensuous joy in getting out of bed, feeling under his bare feet the softness of the sunlit carpet, and entering the shining tiled sanctuary where his great porcelain bath proffered[3] its renovating flood. But then a year ago he could still call up the horror of the communal **plunge** at his earlier lodgings: the listening for other bathers,

2 *formal*: a main road through a town or city
3 *formal*: offer someone something

the dodging of shrouded ladies in "crimping"-pins[4], the cold wait on the landing, the reluctant **descent** into a **blotchy** tin bath, and the effort to identify one's soap and nail-brush among the **promiscuous** implements of ablution[5]. That memory had faded now, and Betton saw only the dark hours to which his blue and white temple of refreshment formed a kind of glittering antechamber[6]. For after his bath came his breakfast, and on the breakfast-tray his letters. His letters!

He remembered – and *that* memory had not faded! – the thrill with which he had opened the first missive[7] in a strange feminine hand: the letter beginning: "I wonder if you'll mind an unknown reader's telling you all that your book has been to her?"

Mind? Ye gods[8], he minded now! For more than a year after the publication of "Diadems and Faggots" the letters, the inane indiscriminate letters of condemnation, of criticism, of interrogation, had poured in on him by every post. Hundreds of unknown readers had told him with **unsparing** detail all that his book had been to them. And the wonder of it was, when all was said and done, that it had really been so little – that when their thick broth of praise was strained through the author's anxious vanity there remained to him so small a sediment of definite specific understanding! No – it was always the same thing, over and over and over again – the same vague gush of adjectives, the same incorrigible tendency to estimate his effort according to each writer's personal preferences, instead of regarding it as a work of art, a thing to be measured by objective standards!

He smiled to think how little, at first, he had felt the vanity of it all. He had found a **savour** even in the grosser evidences of popularity: the advertisements of his book, the daily shower of "clippings[9]", the sense that, when he entered a restaurant or a theatre, people **nudged** each other and said "That's Betton."

---

4 special hair pins used to create small waves in hair
5 *formal, often considered humorous in modern English*: the process of washing yourself, cleaning your teeth etc
6 *old-fashioned*: anteroom, a small room that leads to a larger and more important room
7 *formal, often humorous in modern English*: a letter, especially a long or important one
8 *spoken, old-fashioned*: used for showing that you are very surprised or annoyed
9 articles or pictures you have cut from a newspaper or magazine

Yes, the publicity had been sweet to him – at first. He had been touched by the sympathy of his fellow-men: had thought indulgently of the world, as a better place than the failures and the dyspeptics[10] would acknowledge. And then his success began to submerge him: he **gasped** under the thickening shower of letters. His admirers were really **unappeasable**. And they wanted him to do such **preposterous** things – to give lectures, to head movements, to be tendered[11] receptions, to speak at banquets, to address mothers, to plead for orphans, to go up in balloons, to lead the struggle for sterilized milk. They wanted his photograph for literary supplements, his autograph for **charity bazaars**, his name on committees, literary, educational, and social; above all, they wanted his opinion on everything: on Christianity, Buddhism, tight lacing[12], the drug-habit, democratic government, **female suffrage** and love. Perhaps the chief benefit of this demand was his incidentally learning from it how few opinions he really had: the only one that remained with him was a rooted horror of all forms of correspondence. He had been unutterably thankful when the letters began to fall off.

"Diadems and Faggots" was now two years old, and the moment was at hand when its author might have counted on regaining the blessed shelter of **oblivion** – if only he had not written another book! For it was the worst part of his **plight** that his first success had **goaded** him to the perpetration of this particular folly – that one of the incentives (hideous thought!) to his new work had been the desire to extend and perpetuate his popularity. And this very week the book was to come out, and the letters, the cursed letters, would begin again!

Wistfully, almost **plaintively**, he contemplated the breakfast-tray with which Strett presently appeared. It bore only two notes and the morning journals[13], but he knew that within the

10 literally, a person suffering from indigestion, used to talk about people who complain a lot
11 be formally offered something, here the position of guest of honour at a large gathering of people
12 the practice, which was still common at the time among young women, of wearing very tight corsets (a form of underwear) that were tied with a long lace, in order to make a woman's waist appear very small
13 *mainly US*: daily newspapers

week it would groan under its epistolary[14] burden[15]. The very newspapers flung the fact at him as he opened them.

READY ON MONDAY.
GEOFFREY BETTON'S NEW NOVEL
ABUNDANCE.
BY THE AUTHOR OF "DIADEMS AND FAGGOTS".
FIRST EDITION OF ONE HUNDRED AND FIFTY THOUSAND ALREADY SOLD OUT.
ORDER NOW.

A hundred and fifty thousand volumes! And an average of three readers to each! Half a million of people[16] would be reading him within a week, and every one of them would write to him, and their friends and relations would write too. He laid down the paper with a **shudder**.

The two notes looked harmless enough, and the calligraphy[17] of one was vaguely familiar. He opened the envelope and looked at the signature: Duncan Vyse. He had not seen the name in years – what on earth could Duncan Vyse have to say? He ran over the page and dropped it with a wondering exclamation, which the watchful Strett, re-entering, met by a tentative "Yes, sir?"

"Nothing. Yes – that is – " Betton picked up the note. "There's a gentleman, a Mr. Vyse, coming to see me at ten."

Strett glanced at the clock. "Yes, sir. You'll remember that ten was the hour you appointed for the secretaries to call, sir."

Betton nodded. "I'll see Mr. Vyse first. My clothes, please."

As he got into them, in the state of irritable hurry that had become almost chronic with him, he continued to think about Duncan Vyse. They had seen a lot of each other for the few years after both had left Harvard[18]: the hard happy years when Betton had been **grinding** at his business and Vyse – poor devil! – trying to write. The novelist recalled his friend's attempts with a smile; then the memory of one small volume came back to him. It was a novel: "The Lifted Lamp". There was stuff in

14 *literary*: relating to the writing of letters
15 *literary*: something heavy that you have to carry
16 in modern usage we usually say half a million people
17 *old-fashioned, formal*: handwriting
18 the oldest and one of the most prestigious universities in the USA

that, certainly. He remembered Vyse's **tossing it down** on his table with a gesture of despair when it came back from the last publisher. Betton, taking it up indifferently, had sat **riveted** till daylight. When he ended, the impression was so strong that he said to himself: "I'll tell Apthorn about it – I'll go and see him to-morrow." His own secret literary yearnings gave him a passionate desire to **champion** Vyse, to see him triumph over the ignorance and timidity of the publishers. Apthorn was the youngest of the guild[19], still capable of opinions and the courage of them, a personal friend of Betton's, and, as it happened, the man afterward to become known as the privileged publisher of "Diadems and Faggots". Unluckily the next day something unexpected turned up, and Betton forgot about Vyse and his manuscript. He continued to forget for a month, and then came a note from Vyse, who was ill, and wrote to ask what his friend had done. Betton did not like to say "I've done nothing," so he left the note unanswered, and **vowed** again: "I'll see Apthorn."

The following day he was called to the West on business, and was gone a month. When he came back, there was another note from Vyse, who was still ill, and desperately **hard up**. "I'll take anything for the book, if they'll advance me two hundred dollars." Betton, full of compunction, would gladly have advanced the sum himself; but he was hard up too, and could only swear inwardly: "I'll write to Apthorn." Then he glanced again at the manuscript, and reflected: "No – there are things in it that need explaining. I'd better see him."

Once he went so far as to telephone Apthorn, but the publisher was out. Then he finally and completely forgot.

One Sunday he went out of town, and on his return, rummaging among the papers on his desk, he missed "The Lifted Lamp", which had been gathering dust there for half a year. What the deuce[20] could have become of it? Betton spent a feverish hour in vainly increasing the disorder of his documents,

---

19 normally an association of craftsmen in a particular trade, here, presumably, refers to an association of publishers

20 *old-fashioned*: used in questions for emphasising how surprised or annoyed you are (see *Key vocabulary*)

and then bethought himself of[21] calling the maid-servant, who first indignantly denied having touched anything ("I can see that's true from the dust," Betton **scathingly interjected**), and then mentioned with hauteur that a young lady had called in his absence and asked to be allowed to get a book.

"A lady? Did you let her come up?"

"She said somebody'd sent her."

Vyse, of course – Vyse had sent her for his manuscript! He was always mixed up with some woman, and it was just like him to send the girl of the moment to Betton's lodgings, with instructions to force the door in his absence. Vyse had never been remarkable for delicacy. Betton, furious, glanced over his table to see if any of his own effects were missing – one couldn't tell, with the company Vyse kept! – and then dismissed the matter from his mind, with a vague sense of magnanimity in doing so. He felt himself exonerated[22] by Vyse's conduct.

The sense of magnanimity was still uppermost when the valet opened the door to announce "Mr. Vyse," and Betton, a moment later, crossed the threshold of his pleasant library.

His first thought was that the man facing him from the hearth-rug was the very Duncan Vyse of old: small, starved, bleached-looking, with the same sidelong movements, the same queer[23] air of anaemic truculence. Only he had grown shabbier, and bald.

Betton held out a hospitable hand.

"This is a good surprise! Glad you looked me up, my dear fellow."

Vyse's palm was damp and bony: he had always had a disagreeable hand.

"You got my note? You know what I've come for?" he said.

"About the secretaryship? (Sit down.) Is that really serious?"

Betton lowered himself luxuriously into one of his vast Maple arm-chairs. He had grown **stouter** in the last year, and the cushion behind him fitted comfortably into the crease of

21 *old-fashioned*: thought about
22 *formal*: officially cleared, or freed, of guilt
23 *old-fashioned*: strange

his **nape**. As he leaned back he caught sight of his image in the mirror between the windows, and reflected uneasily that Vyse would not find *him* unchanged.

"Serious?" Vyse rejoined. "Why not? Aren't *you*?"

"Oh, perfectly." Betton laughed apologetically. "Only – well, the fact is, you may not understand what rubbish a secretary of mine would have to deal with. In advertising for one I never imagined – I didn't aspire to any one above the ordinary hack[24]."

"I'm the ordinary hack," said Vyse drily.

Betton's **affable** gesture protested. "My dear fellow – . You see it's not business – what I'm in now," he continued with a laugh.

Vyse's thin lips seemed to form a noiseless "*Isn't* it?" which they instantly transposed into the audible reply: "I inferred from your advertisement that you want someone to relieve you in your literary work. Dictation, short-hand[25] – that kind of thing?"

"Well, no: not that either. I type my own things. What I'm looking for is somebody who won't be above tackling my correspondence."

Vyse looked slightly surprised. "I should be glad of the job," he then said.

Betton began to feel a vague embarrassment. He had supposed that such a proposal would be instantly rejected. "It would be only for an hour or two a day – if you're doing any writing of your own?" he threw out interrogatively.

"No. I've given all that up. I'm in an office now – business. But it doesn't take all my time, or pay enough to keep me alive."

"In that case, my dear fellow – if you could come every morning; but it's mostly awful bosh[26], you know," Betton again broke off, with growing awkwardness.

Vyse glanced at him humorously. "What you want me to write?"

---

24 *informal*: a journalist, artist or writer who does boring work or work that isn't very good
25 a quick way of writing that uses symbols to represent letters, words or phrases, used especially when you write what someone is saying as they are talking
26 *old-fashioned*: nonsense

Full Circle | 157

"Well, that depends – " Betton sketched the obligatory smile. "But I was thinking of the letters you'll have to answer. Letters about my books, you know – I've another one appearing next week. And I want to be beforehand now – **dam** the flood before it **swamps** me. Have you any idea of the **deluge** of stuff that people write to a successful novelist?"

As Betton spoke, he saw a tinge of red on Vyse's thin cheek, and his own reflected it in a richer glow of shame. "I mean – I mean – " he **stammered** helplessly.

"No, I haven't," said Vyse; "but it will be awfully jolly finding out."

There was a pause, groping and desperate on Betton's part, **sardonically** calm on his visitor's.

"You – you've given up writing altogether?" Betton continued.

"Yes; we've changed places, as it were." Vyse paused. "But about these letters – you dictate the answers?"

"Lord, no! That's the reason why I said I wanted somebody – er – well used to writing. I don't want to have anything to do with them – not a thing! You'll have to answer them as if they were written to *you* – " Betton pulled himself up again, and rising in confusion **jerked open** one of the drawers of his writing-table.

"Here – this kind of rubbish," he said, tossing a packet of letters onto Vyse's knee.

"Oh – you keep them, do you?" said Vyse simply.

"I – well – some of them; a few of the funniest only."

Vyse slipped off the band and began to open the letters. While he was glancing over them Betton again caught his own reflection in the glass, and asked himself what impression he had made on his visitor. It occurred to him for the first time that his **high-coloured** well-fed person presented the image of commercial rather than of intellectual achievement. He did not look like his own idea of the author of "Diadems and Faggots" – and he wondered why.

Vyse laid the letters aside. "I think I can do it – if you'll give me a notion of the tone I'm to take."

"The tone?"

"Yes – that is, if I'm to sign your name."

"Oh, of course: I expect you to sign for me. As for the tone, say just what you'd – well, say all you can without encouraging them to answer."

Vyse rose from his seat. "I could submit a few **specimens**," he suggested.

"Oh, as to that – you always wrote better than I do," said Betton handsomely.

"I've never had this kind of thing to write. When do you wish me to begin?" Vyse enquired, ignoring the tribute.

"The book's out on Monday. The deluge will begin about three days after. Will you turn up on Thursday at this hour?" Betton held his hand out with real **heartiness**. "It was great luck for me, your striking[27] that advertisement. Don't be too harsh with my correspondents – I owe them something for having brought us together."

II

The deluge began punctually on the Thursday, and Vyse, arriving as punctually, had an impressive pile of letters to attack. Betton, on his way to the Park for a ride, came into the library, smoking the cigarette of indolence[28], to look over his secretary's shoulder.

"How many of 'em[29]? Twenty? Good Lord! It's going to be worse than "Diadems". I've just had my first quiet breakfast in two years – time to read the papers and loaf[30]. How I used to dread the sight of my letter-box! Now I sha'n't[31] know I have one."

He leaned over Vyse's chair, and the secretary handed him a letter.

"Here's rather an exceptional one – lady, evidently. I thought you might want to answer it yourself – "

27 usually used with the preposition on, to strike on something, to notice something
28 *formal*: laziness
29 *spoken*: them
30 *informal*: spend time doing nothing, usually when you should be working
31 shall not

"Exceptional?" Betton ran over the **mauve** pages and tossed them down. "Why, my dear man, I get hundreds like that. You'll have to be pretty short with her, or she'll send her photograph."

He clapped Vyse on the shoulder and turned away, humming a tune. "Stay to luncheon[32]," he called back gaily from the threshold.

After luncheon Vyse insisted on showing a few of his answers to the first batch of letters. "If I've struck the note I won't bother you again," he urged; and Betton **groaningly** consented.

"My dear fellow, they're beautiful – too beautiful. I'll be let in for a correspondence with every one of these people."

Vyse, at this, meditated for a while above a blank sheet. "All right – how's this?" he said, after another interval of rapid writing.

Betton glanced over the page. "By George – by George[33]! Won't she *see* it?" he exulted, between fear and rapture.

"It's wonderful how little people see," said Vyse reassuringly. The letters continued to pour in for several weeks after the appearance of "Abundance". For five or six blissful days Betton did not even have his mail brought to him, trusting to Vyse to single out his personal correspondence, and to deal with the rest according to their agreement. During those days he luxuriated in a sense of wild and lawless freedom; then, gradually, he began to feel the need of fresh restraints to break, and learned that the zest of liberty lies in the escape from specific obligations. At first he was conscious only of a vague hunger, but in time the **craving** resolved into a **shame-faced** desire to see his letters.

"After all, I hated them only because I had to answer them"; and he told Vyse carelessly that he wished all his letters submitted to him before the secretary answered them.

At first he pushed aside those beginning: "I have just laid down 'Abundance' after a third reading," or: "Every day for the last month I have been telephoning my bookseller to know when your novel would be out." But little by little the freshness

32 *formal*: lunch, especially a formal lunch (see *Key vocabulary*)
33 *old-fashioned*: exclamation used to express surprise (see *Key vocabulary*)

of his interest revived, and even this stereotyped homage began to arrest his eye. At last a day came when he read all the letters, from the first word to the last, as he had done when "Diadems and Faggots" appeared. It was really a pleasure to read them, now that he was relieved of the burden of replying: his new relation to his correspondents had the glow of a love-affair unchilled by the contingency[34] of marriage.

One day it struck him that the letters were coming in more slowly and in smaller numbers. Certainly there had been more of a rush when "Diadems and Faggots" came out. Betton began to wonder if Vyse were exercising an unauthorized discrimination, and keeping back the communications he **deemed** least important. This sudden **conjecture** carried the novelist straight to his library, where he found Vyse bending over the writing-table with his usual **inscrutable** pale smile. But once there, Betton hardly knew how to frame his question, and blundered into an enquiry for a missing invitation.

"There's a note – a personal note – I ought to have had this morning. Sure you haven't kept it back by mistake among the others?"

Vyse laid down his pen. "The others? But I never keep back any."

Betton had foreseen the answer. "Not even the worst twaddle[35] about my book?" he suggested lightly, pushing the papers about.

"Nothing. I understood you wanted to go over them all first."

"Well, perhaps it's safer," Betton conceded, as if the idea were new to him. With an embarrassed hand he continued to turn over the letters at Vyse's elbow.

"Those are yesterday's," said the secretary; "here are to-day's," he added, pointing to a meagre trio.

"H'm – only these?" Betton took them and looked them over **lingeringly**. "I don't see what the deuce that chap means about the first part of 'Abundance' 'certainly justifying the title' – do you?"

34 possibility
35 *informal*: nonsense

Vyse was silent, and the novelist continued irritably: "Damned[36] cheek, his writing, if he doesn't like the book. Who cares what he thinks about it, anyhow?"

And his morning ride was **embittered** by the discovery that it was unexpectedly disagreeable to have Vyse read any letters which did not express unqualified praise of his books. He began to fancy there was a **latent** rancour, a kind of **baffled sneer**, under Vyse's manner; and he decided to return to the practice of having his mail brought straight to his room. In that way he could edit the letters before his secretary saw them.

Vyse made no comment on the change, and Betton was reduced to wondering whether his **imperturbable** composure were the mask of complete indifference or of a watchful jealousy. The latter view being more agreeable to his employer's self-esteem, the next step was to conclude that Vyse had not forgotten the episode of "The Lifted Lamp", and would naturally take a **vindictive** joy in any unfavourable judgments passed on his rival's work. This did not simplify the situation, for there was no denying that unfavourable criticisms **preponderated**[37] in Betton's correspondence. "Abundance" was neither meeting with the unrestricted welcome of "Diadems and Faggots", nor enjoying the alternative of an animated controversy: it was simply found dull, and its readers said so in language not too tactfully **tempered** by regretful comparisons with its predecessor. To withhold unfavourable comments from Vyse was, therefore, to make it appear that correspondence about the book had died out; and its author, **mindful of** his **unguarded** predictions, found this even more embarrassing. The simplest solution would be to get rid of Vyse; and to this end Betton began to address his energies.

One evening, finding himself unexpectedly disengaged, he asked Vyse to dine; it had occurred to him that, in the course of an after-dinner chat, he might delicately hint his feeling that the work he had offered his friend was **unworthy** of so **accomplished** a hand.

36 impolite, showing annoyance
37 *formal*: to be most common

Vyse surprised him by a momentary hesitation. "I may not have time to dress[38]."

Betton stared. "What's the odds? We'll dine here – and as late as you like."

Vyse thanked him, and appeared, punctually at eight, in all the **shabbiness** of his daily wear. He looked paler and more shyly truculent[39] than usual, and Betton, from the height of his florid[40] stature, said to himself, with the sudden professional instinct for "type": "He might be an agent of something – a chap who carries deadly secrets."

Vyse, it was to appear, did carry a deadly secret; but one less perilous to society than to himself. He was simply poor – inexcusably, irremediably poor. Everything failed him, had always failed him: whatever he put his hand to went to bits.

This was the confession that, reluctantly, yet with a kind of white-lipped **bravado**, he flung at Betton in answer to the latter's tentative suggestion that, really, the letter-answering job wasn't worth bothering him with – a thing that any type-writer could do.

"If you mean you're paying me more than it's worth, I'll take less," Vyse rushed out after a pause.

"Oh, my dear fellow – " Betton protested, flushing.

"What do you mean, then? Don't I answer the letters as you want them answered?"

Betton anxiously stroked his silken ankle. "You do it beautifully, too beautifully. I mean what I say: the work's not worthy of you. I'm ashamed to ask you – "

"Oh, hang shame," Vyse interrupted. "Do you know why I said I shouldn't have time to dress to-night? Because I haven't any evening clothes. As a matter of fact, I haven't much but the clothes I stand in. One thing after another's gone against me; all the infernal ingenuities of chance. It's been a slow Chinese torture, the kind where they keep you alive to have more fun killing you." He straightened himself with a sudden blush. "Oh, I'm all right now – getting on capitally. But I'm still walking

38 change into formal evening dress

39 *formal*: easily annoyed and always ready to argue or fight

40 red-faced

rather a narrow plank[41]; and if I do your work well enough – if I take your idea – "

Betton stared into the fire without answering. He knew next to nothing of Vyse's history, of the mischance or mis-management that had brought him, with his brains and his training, to so unlikely a pass[42]. But a pang of compunction shot through him as he remembered the manuscript of "The Lifted Lamp" gathering dust on his table for half a year.

"Not that it would have made any earthly difference – since he's evidently never been able to get the thing published." But this reflection did not wholly console Betton, and he found it impossible, at the moment, to tell Vyse that his services were not needed.

III

During the ensuing weeks the letters grew fewer and fewer, and Betton foresaw the approach of the fatal day when his secretary, in common decency[43], would have to say: "I can't draw my pay for doing nothing."

What a triumph for Vyse!

The thought was intolerable, and Betton cursed his weakness in not having dismissed the fellow before such a possibility arose.

"If I tell him I've no use for him now, he'll see straight through it, of course; – and then, hang it, he looks so poor!"

This consideration came after the other, but Betton, in rearranging them, put it first, because he thought it looked better there, and also because he immediately perceived its value in justifying a plan of action that was beginning to take shape in his mind.

"Poor devil, I'm damned if I don't do it for him!" said Betton, sitting down at his desk.

Three or four days later he sent word to Vyse that he didn't care to go over the letters any longer, and that they would once

41 in a dangerous position; metaphor taken from the practice of making prisoners walk off a ship along a long plank of wood and into the sea to drown
42 come/bring to a pass: used for saying that a situation has become very unpleasant or difficult
43 *phrase*: standard of good behaviour that everyone should have

more be carried directly to the library.

The next time he lounged in, on his way to his morning ride, he found his secretary's pen in active motion.

"A lot to-day," Vyse told him cheerfully.

His tone irritated Betton: it had the **inane** optimism of the physician reassuring a discouraged patient.

"Oh, Lord – I thought it was almost over," groaned the novelist.

"No: they've just got their second wind. Here's one from a Chicago publisher – never heard the name – offering you thirty per cent. On your next novel, with an advance royalty of twenty thousand. And here's a chap who wants to syndicate[44] it for a bunch of Sunday papers: big offer, too. That's from Ann Arbor. And this – oh, *this* one's funny!"

He held up a small scented sheet to Betton, who made no movement to receive it.

"Funny? Why's it funny?" he **growled**.

"Well, it's from a girl – a lady – and she thinks she's the only person who understands 'Abundance' – has the clue to it. Says she's never seen a book so misrepresented by the critics – "

"Ha, ha! That is good!" Betton agreed with too loud a laugh.

"This one's from a lady, too – married woman. Says she's misunderstood, and would like to correspond."

"Oh, Lord," said Betton. "What are you looking at?" he added sharply, as Vyse continued to bend his blinking gaze on the letters.

"I was only thinking I'd never seen such short letters from women. Neither one fills the first page."

"Well, what of that?" queried Betton.

Vyse reflected. "I'd like to meet a woman like that," he said wearily; and Betton laughed again.

The letters continued to pour in, and there could be no farther question of dispensing with Vyse's services. But one morning, about three weeks later, the latter asked for a word with his employer, and Betton, on entering the library, found his

---

44 buy the rights to the story in order to be able to publish it in a number of different newspapers

secretary with half a dozen documents spread out before him.

"What's up?" queried Betton, with a touch of impatience.

Vyse was attentively scanning the outspread letters.

"I don't know: can't make out." His voice had a faint note of embarrassment. "Do you remember a note signed *Hester Macklin* that came three or four weeks ago? Married – misunderstood – Western army post – wanted to correspond?"

Betton seemed to **grope** among his memories; then he **assented** vaguely.

"A short note," Vyse went on: "the whole story in half a page. The shortness struck me so much – and the directness – that I wrote her[45]: wrote in my own name, I mean."

"In your own name?" Betton stood amazed; then he broke into a **groan**.

"Good Lord, Vyse – you're **incorrigible**!"

The secretary pulled his thin moustache with a nervous laugh. "If you mean I'm an ass, you're right. Look here." He held out an envelope stamped with the words: "Dead Letter Office." "My effusion[46] has come back to me marked 'unknown.' There's no such person at the address she gave you."

Betton seemed for an instant to share his secretary's embarrassment; then he burst into an **uproarious** laugh.

"Hoax[47], was it? That's rough on you, old fellow!"

Vyse shrugged his shoulders. "Yes; but the interesting question is – why on earth didn't *your* answer come back, too?"

"My answer?"

"The official one – the one I wrote in your name. If she's unknown, what's become of *that*?"

Betton stared at him with eyes wrinkled by amusement. "Perhaps she hadn't disappeared then."

Vyse disregarded the conjecture. "Look here – I believe *all* these letters are a hoax," he broke out.

Betton stared at him with a face that turned slowly red and angry. "What are you talking about? All what letters?"

45 US English: in British English we use the preposition to; *I wrote to her*
46 *mainly literary*: an act of expressing feelings in an extremely enthusiastic way
47 false – not written by the person who has signed their name

"These I've spread out here: I've been comparing them. And I believe they're all written by one man."

Burton's redness turned to a purple that made his **ruddy**[48] moustache seem pale. "What the devil are you driving at?" he asked.

"Well, just look at it," Vyse persisted, still bent above the letters. "I've been studying them carefully – those that have come within the last two or three weeks – and there's a queer likeness in the writing of some of them. The g's are all like corkscrews. And the same phrases keep recurring – the Ann Arbor news-agent uses the same expressions as the President of the Girls' College at Euphorbia, Maine."

Betton laughed. "Aren't the critics always groaning over the **shrinkage** of the national vocabulary? Of course we all use the same expressions."

"Yes," said Vyse obstinately. "But how about using the same g's?"

Betton laughed again, but Vyse continued without heeding him: "Look here, Betton – could Strett have written them?"

"Strett?" Betton roared. "*Strett?*" He threw himself into his arm-chair to shake out his mirth at greater ease.

"I'll tell you why. Strett always posts all my answers. He comes in for them every day before I leave. He posted the letter to the misunderstood party – the letter from *you* that the Dead Letter Office didn't return. *I* posted my own letter to her; and that came back."

A measurable silence followed the emission of this ingenious conjecture; then Betton observed with gentle irony: "Extremely neat. And of course it's no business of yours to supply any valid motive for this remarkable attention on my valet's part."

Vyse cast on him a slanting glance.

"If you've found that human conduct's generally based on valid motives – !"

"Well, outside of mad-houses it's supposed to be not quite incalculable."

48 *literary*: red

Vyse had an odd smile under his thin moustache. "Every house is a mad-house at some time or another."

Betton rose with a careless shake of the shoulders. "This one will be if I talk to you much longer," he said, moving away with a laugh.

IV

Betton did not for a moment believe that Vyse suspected the valet of having written the letters.

"Why the devil don't he say out what he thinks? He was always a tortuous chap," he grumbled inwardly.

The sense of being held under the lens of Vyse's mute scrutiny became more and more exasperating. Betton, by this time, had squared his shoulders to the fact that "Abundance" was a failure with the public: a confessed and glaring failure. The press told him so openly, and his friends emphasized the fact by their circumlocutions and evasions. Betton minded it a good deal more than he had expected, but not nearly as much as he minded Vyse's knowing it. That remained the central **twinge** in his diffused discomfort. And the problem of getting rid of his secretary once more engaged him.

He had set aside all sentimental pretexts for retaining Vyse; but a practical argument replaced them. "If I ship him[49] now he'll think it's because I'm ashamed to have him see that I'm not getting any more letters."

For the letters had ceased again, almost abruptly, since Vyse had hazarded the conjecture that they were the product of Strett's devoted pen. Betton had reverted only once to the subject – to ask ironically, a day or two later: "Is Strett writing to me as much as ever?" – and, on Vyse's replying with a neutral head-shake, had added with a laugh: "If you suspect *him* you might as well think I write the letters myself!"

"There are very few to-day," said Vyse, with his irritating evasiveness; and Betton rejoined squarely: "Oh, they'll stop soon. The book's a failure."

A few mornings later he felt a rush of shame at his own

---

49 *informal*: get rid of him

tergiversations[50], and stalked into the library with Vyse's sentence on his tongue.

Vyse started back with one of his anaemic blushes. "I was hoping you'd be in. I wanted to speak to you. There've been no letters the last day or two," he explained.

Betton drew a quick breath of relief. The man had some sense of decency, then! He meant to dismiss himself.

"I told you so, my dear fellow; the book's a flat failure," he said, almost gaily.

Vyse made a deprecating gesture. "I don't know that I should regard the absence of letters as the ultimate test. But I wanted to ask you if there isn't something else I can do on the days when there's no writing." He turned his glance toward the book-lined walls. "Don't you want your library catalogued?" he asked **insidiously**.

"Had it done last year, thanks." Betton glanced away from Vyse's face. It was piteous, how he needed the job!

"I see. ... Of course this is just a temporary **lull** in the letters. They'll begin again – as they did before. The people who read carefully read slowly – you haven't heard yet what *they* think."

Betton felt a rush of **puerile** joy at the suggestion. Actually, he hadn't thought of that!

"There *was* a big second crop after 'Diadems and Faggots,'" he mused aloud.

"Of course. Wait and see," said Vyse confidently.

The letters in fact began again – more gradually and in smaller numbers. But their quality was different, as Vyse had predicted. And in two cases Betton's correspondents, not content to compress into one rapid communication the thoughts inspired by his work, developed their views in a succession of really remarkable letters. One of the writers was a professor in a Western college; the other was a girl in Florida. In their language, their point of view, their reasons for appreciating "Abundance," they differed almost **diametrically**; but this only made the unanimity of their approval the more striking. The rush of correspondence evoked

---

50 *unusual, formal*: evasions and ambiguities

by Betton's earlier novel had produced nothing so personal, so exceptional as these communications. He had gulped the praise of "Diadems and Faggots" as undiscriminatingly as it was offered; now he knew for the first time the subtler pleasures of the palate. He tried to **feign** indifference, even to himself; and to Vyse he made no sign. But gradually he felt a desire to know what his secretary thought of the letters, and, above all, what he was saying in reply to them. And he resented acutely the possibility of Vyse's starting one of his clandestine correspondences with the girl in Florida. Vyse's notorious lack of delicacy had never been more vividly present to Betton's imagination; and he made up his mind to answer the letters himself.

He would keep Vyse on, of course: there were other communications that the secretary could attend to. And, if necessary, Betton would invent an occupation: he cursed his stupidity in having betrayed the fact that his books were already catalogued.

Vyse showed no surprise when Betton announced his intention of dealing personally with the two correspondents who showed so flattering a reluctance to take their leave. But Betton immediately read a criticism in his lack of comment, and put forth, on a note of challenge: "After all, one must be decent!"

Vyse looked at him with an evanescent[51] smile. "You'll have to explain that you didn't write the first answers."

Betton halted. "Well – I – I more or less dictated them, didn't I?"

"Oh, virtually, they're yours, of course."

"You think I can put it that way?"

"Why not?" The secretary absently drew an arabesque[52] on the blotting-pad. "Of course they'll keep it up longer if you write yourself," he suggested.

Betton blushed, but faced the issue. "Hang it all, I sha'n't be sorry. They interest me. They're remarkable letters." And Vyse, without observation, returned to his writings.

51 *mainly literary*: lasting for only a very short time
52 a pattern of curved lines

The spring, that year, was delicious to Betton. His college professor continued to address him tersely but cogently[53] at fixed intervals, and twice a week eight serried[54] pages came from Florida. There were other letters, too; he had the **solace** of feeling that at last "Abundance" was making its way, was reaching the people who, as Vyse said, read slowly because they read intelligently. But welcome as were all these proofs of his restored authority they were but the background of his happiness. His life revolved for the moment about the personality of his two chief correspondents. The professor's letters satisfied his craving for intellectual recognition, and the satisfaction he felt in them proved how completely he had lost faith in himself. He blushed to think that his opinion of his work had been **swayed** by the **shallow** judgments of a public whose taste he despised. Was it possible that he had allowed himself to think less well of "Abundance" because it was not to the taste of the average novel-reader? Such false humility was less excusable than the crudest appetite for praise: it was ridiculous to try to do conscientious work if one's self-esteem were at the mercy of popular judgments. All this the professor's letters delicately and indirectly conveyed to Betton, with the result that the author of "Abundance" began to recognize in it the ripest flower of his genius.

But if the professor understood his book, the girl in Florida understood *him*; and Betton was fully alive to the superior qualities of discernment[55] which this process implied. For his lovely correspondent his novel was but the starting-point, the pretext of her discourse: he himself was her real object, and he had the delicious sense, as their exchange of thoughts proceeded, that she was interested in "Abundance" because of its author, rather than in the author because of his book. Of course she laid stress on the fact that his ideas were the object of her contemplation; but Betton's agreeable person had permitted him some insight into the incorrigible subjectiveness of female judgments, and he was pleasantly aware, from the lady's tone, that she guessed him

53 *formal*: in a reasoned and sensible way
54 *literary*: written in lines arranged very closely together
55 the ability to make good judgements about things such as art and literature

to be neither old nor ridiculous. And suddenly he wrote to ask if he might see her. ...

The answer was long in coming. Betton **fumed** at the delay, watched, wondered, **fretted**; then he received the one word "Impossible."

He wrote back more urgently, and awaited the reply with increasing eagerness. A certain shyness had kept him from once more modifying the instructions regarding his mail, and Strett still carried the letters directly to Vyse. The hour when he knew they were passing under the latter's eyes was now becoming intolerable to Betton, and it was a profound relief when the secretary, suddenly advised of his father's illness, asked permission to absent himself for a fortnight.

Vyse departed just after Betton had despatched to Florida his second missive of entreaty[56], and for ten days he tasted the **furtive** joy of a first perusal[57] of his letters. The answer from Florida was not among them; but Betton said to himself "She's thinking it over," and delay, in that light, seemed favourable. So charming, in fact, was this phase of sentimental suspense that he felt a start of resentment when a telegram apprised[58] him one morning that Vyse would return to his post that day.

Betton had slept later than usual, and, springing out of bed with the telegram in his hand, he learned from the clock that his secretary was due in half an hour. He reflected that the morning's mail must long since be in; and, too impatient to wait for its appearance with his breakfast-tray, he threw on a dressing-gown and went to the library. There lay the letters, half a dozen of them: but his eye flew to one envelope, and as he tore it open a warm wave rocked his heart.

The letter was dated a few days after its writer must have received his own: it had all the qualities of grace and insight to which his unknown friend had accustomed him, but it contained no allusion, however indirect, to the special purport[59]

56 *formal, phrase 'missive of entreaty'*: a strong serious request that you make to someone about something that is worrying you
57 *formal*: the act of reading something
58 *formal*: tell someone about something
59 *very formal*: the basic meaning of a statement or document

of his appeal. Even a vanity less ingenious than Betton's might have read in the lady's silence one of the most familiar motions of consent; but the smile provoked by this inference faded as he turned to his other letters. For the uppermost bore the superscription "Dead Letter Office," and the document that fell from it was his own last letter from Florida.

Betton studied the ironic "Unknown" for an appreciable space of time; then he broke into a laugh. He had suddenly recalled Vyse's similar experience with "Hester Macklin," and the light he was able to throw on that obscure episode was searching enough to penetrate all the dark corners of his own adventure. He felt a rush of heat to the ears; catching sight of himself in the glass, he saw a red ridiculous **congested** countenance, and dropped into a chair to hide it between flushed fists. He was roused by the opening of the door, and Vyse appeared on the threshold.

"Oh, I beg pardon – you're ill?" said the secretary.

Betton's only answer was an inarticulate murmur of derision; then he pushed forward the letter with the imprint of the Dead Letter Office.

"Look at that," he **jeered**.

Vyse peered at the envelope, and turned it over slowly in his hands. Betton's eyes, fixed on him, saw his face decompose like a substance touched by some powerful acid. He clung to the envelope as if to gain time.

"It's from the young lady you've been writing to at Swazee Springs?" he asked at length.

"It's from the young lady I've been writing to at Swazee Springs."

"Well – I suppose she's gone away," continued Vyse, rebuilding his countenance[60] rapidly.

"Yes; and in a community numbering perhaps a hundred and seventy-five souls, including the dogs and chickens, the local post-office is so ignorant of her movements that my letter has to be sent to the Dead Letter Office."

---

60 *literary*: your face, or the expression on your face

Vyse meditated on this; then he laughed in turn. "After all, the same thing happened to me – with 'Hester Macklin,' I mean," he recalled **sheepishly**.

"Just so," said Betton, bringing down his clenched fist on the table. "*Just so*," he repeated, in italics.

He caught his secretary's glance, and held it with his own for a moment. Then he dropped it as, in pity, one releases something scared and squirming.

"The very day my letter was returned from Swazee Springs she wrote me this from there," he said, holding up the last Florida missive.

"Ha! That's funny," said Vyse, with a damp forehead.

"Yes, it's funny; it's funny," said Betton. He leaned back, his hands in his pockets, staring up at the ceiling, and noticing a crack in the cornice[61]. Vyse, at the corner of the writing-table, waited.

"Shall I get to work?" he began, after a silence measurable by minutes. Betton's gaze descended from the cornice.

"I've got your seat, haven't I?" he said, rising and moving away from the table.

Vyse, with a quick gleam of relief, slipped into the vacant chair, and began to stir about vaguely among the papers.

"How's your father?" Betton asked from the **hearth**.

"Oh, better – better, thank you. He'll pull out of it."

"But you had a sharp scare for a day or two?"

"Yes – it was touch and go when I got there."

Another pause, while Vyse began to classify the letters.

"And I suppose," Betton continued in a steady tone, "your anxiety made you forget your usual precautions – whatever they were – about this Florida correspondence, and before you'd had time to prevent it the Swazee post-office blundered?"

Vyse lifted his head with a quick movement. "What do you mean?" he asked, pushing his chair back.

"I mean that you saw I couldn't live without flattery, and that you've been ladling it out to me to earn your keep."

---

61 a raised line of plaster, wood or stone at the edge of the ceiling

Vyse sat motionless and shrunken, digging the blotting-pad[62] with his pen. "What on earth are you driving at?" he repeated.

"Though why the deuce," Betton continued in the same steady tone, "you should need to do this kind of work when you've got such faculties at your service – those letters were magnificent, my dear fellow! Why in the world don't you write novels, instead of writing to other people about them?"

Vyse straightened himself with an effort. "What are you talking about, Betton? Why the devil do you think *I* wrote those letters?"

Betton held back his answer, with a brooding face. "Because I wrote 'Hester Macklin's' – to myself!"

Vyse sat **stock-still**, without the least outcry of wonder. "Well – ?" he finally said, in a low tone.

"And because you found me out (you see, you can't even feign surprise!) – because you saw through it at a glance, knew at once that the letters were **faked**. And when you'd foolishly put me on my guard by pointing out to me that they were a clumsy **forgery**, and had then suddenly guessed that *I* was the **forger,** you drew the natural inference that I had to have popular approval, or at least had to make *you* think I had it. You saw that, to me, the worst thing about the failure of the book was having *you* know it was a failure. And so you applied your superior – your immeasurably superior – abilities to carrying on the **humbug**, and deceiving me as I'd tried to deceive you. And you did it so successfully that I don't see why the devil you haven't made your fortune writing novels!"

Vyse remained silent, his head slightly bent under the mounting tide of Betton's **denunciation**.

"The way you differentiated your people – characterised them – avoided my stupid mistake of making the women's letters too short and logical, of letting my different correspondents use the same expressions: the amount of ingenuity and art you wasted on it! I swear, Vyse, I'm sorry that damned post-office went back on you," Betton went on, piling up the waves of his irony.

62 special thick paper used for drying ink

Full Circle | 175

But at this height they suddenly paused, drew back on themselves, and began to recede before the spectacle of Vyse's pale distress. Something warm and emotional in Betton's nature – a lurking kindliness, perhaps, for any one who tried to soothe and smooth his writhing ego – softened his eye as it rested on the drooping figure of his secretary.

"Look here, Vyse – I'm not sorry – not altogether sorry this has happened!" He moved slowly across the room, and laid a friendly palm on Vyse's shoulder. "In a queer illogical way it evens up things, as it were. I did you a **shabby** turn once, years ago – oh, out of sheer carelessness, of course – about that novel of yours I promised to give to Apthorn. If I *had* given it, it might not have made any difference – I'm not sure it wasn't too good for success – but anyhow, I dare say you thought my personal influence might have helped you, might at least have got you a quicker hearing. Perhaps you thought it was because the thing *was* so good that I kept it back, that I felt some nasty jealousy of your superiority. I swear to you it wasn't that – I clean forgot it. And one day when I came home it was gone: you'd sent and taken it. And I've always thought since you might have owed me a **grudge** – and not unjustly; so this ... this business of the letters ... the sympathy you've shown ... for I suppose it *is* sympathy ... ?"

Vyse startled and checked him by a queer **crackling** laugh.

"It's *not* sympathy?" broke in Betton, the moisture drying out of his voice. He withdrew his hand from Vyse's shoulder. "What is it, then? The joy of uncovering my nakedness? An eye for an eye? Is it that?"

Vyse rose from his seat, and with a mechanical gesture swept into a heap all the letters he had sorted.

"I'm stone broke, and wanted to keep my job – that's what it is," he said wearily ...

Post-reading exercises

Understanding the story

1 Use these questions to help you check that you have understood the story.

I

1 Where is Geoffrey Betton at the beginning of the story?
2 What had the valet been doing while Betton was still asleep?
3 What noises can Betton hear through his open window?
4 How does he feel about the noises? Why?
5 What differences does he describe between the way he used to live and the way he lives now?
6 What caused the change in his lifestyle?
7 Who wrote the letters?
8 Why did they write them?
9 How did Betton feel about the letters at the beginning?
10 What other aspects of his newfound fame did he enjoy?
11 What aspects did he not enjoy so much?
12 Why did he write a second book?
13 How does he feel about the imminent appearance of the second book?
14 Who is Duncan Vyse?
15 Why has he written to Geoffrey Betton?
16 How had Betton offered to help Vyse when they were younger?
17 Why didn't he keep his promise?
18 What might have happened if Betton had done what he had promised to do?
19 Was Betton pleased to see Vyse when he arrived?
20 Had Vyse changed since Betton had last seen him?
21 How had Betton changed?
22 What does Betton want his secretary to do for him?
23 Why does he think Vyse might not be interested in the job?
24 Why does Vyse want the job?
25 Why does Betton feel embarrassed about offering the job to his old friend?

II

26 How many letters did Betton receive on the first day?
27 Where did Betton go while Vyse answered the letters?
28 Why did Vyse show Betton some of the letters he had written?

29 What changes did he make?
30 Was Betton pleased with Vyse's work?
31 Why did Betton ask to see his letters at the end of the first week?
32 Why did he enjoy reading them so much?
33 What does Betton think is happening when fewer letters start to arrive?
34 Why does he ask Vyse if he is keeping back some of his mail?
35 Why has his attitude to the letters changed?
36 Why does he decide to look at the letters himself before giving them to Vyse? What is he worried about?
37 Why does Betton think Vyse might be jealous?
38 Why does he invite Vyse to have dinner with him?
39 Why does Vyse hesitate before accepting the invitation?
40 What confession does Vyse make over dinner?
41 Why does Betton feel guilty?

III

42 Why is Betton worried about the fact that there are fewer and fewer letters arriving?
43 Why doesn't he want to tell Vyse that he doesn't need him any more?
44 What is Betton's plan?
45 Why is Vyse suddenly busy?
46 Why does he show two of the letters to Betton? What is strange about them?
47 Who is Hester Macklin?
48 Why did Vyse write to her in his own name?
49 What happened to his reply?
50 Why does Vyse think the letters are a hoax?
51 Who does he think wrote the letters?
52 What is Betton's reaction to Vyse's theory?

IV

53 How does Betton feel about the failure of his second novel?
54 How does Vyse feel about the absence of letters to answer?
55 What reason does Vyse give Betton for the possibility of a second wave of letters?
56 In what way is the second wave of letters different from the first?
57 Why does Betton decide to start answering the letters himself?
58 Why does he enjoy the professor's letters so much?
59 Why does he want to meet the girl in Florida?
60 What was the girl's reply to his suggestion?

61 Why didn't Betton accept her reply?
62 Why did Vyse have to go away?
63 Why did Betton enjoy his absence?
64 What did he do on the morning that Vyse was returning to work?
65 What did he find in his mail?
66 What conclusion does he reach?
67 What explanation does Vyse offer?
68 What does Betton accuse Vyse of doing?
69 What does Betton think were Vyse's motives?
70 How does Vyse react to Betton's accusations and explanations?
71 What is Vyse's real motive?

Language study

Vocabulary

Common metaphors

The use of metaphors is very common in English, as it is in all languages. A metaphor is a type of comparison which uses one concept or idea to describe another. Look at these examples below where relationships are described using the language of temperature or weather.

> *They greeted us **warmly**.*
> *It was a very **stormy** relationship.*

The words in bold are not used with their literal meaning, but with a metaphorical meaning, transferring the image, sensation and associations of warm or stormy weather to the human relationships being described.

In the story, the author makes repeated use of two metaphors that are particularly common in English.

Quantity described in terms of water or rain

On several occasions the author uses words associated with water to describe the number of fan letters that Betton receives after the publication of his two novels.

1 **Look at the key words associated with rain and water. Underline them in the extracts from the story.**

   What image is being created? If it helps you, draw a simple sketch of the image. What is the effect of the metaphor in each example?

> **deluge** (n) a very heavy fall of rain
> **flood** (n) a large amount of water that covers an area that was dry before
> **gush** (n) a large quantity of water that quickly flows out of a place
> **pour** (v) to rain very hard
> **shower** (n) a flow of water that you stand under to wash yourself or a short period of heavy rain
> **submerge** (v) to put something completely under water
> **swamp** (v) to fill or cover something with water

*It was always the same thing, over and over and over again – the same vague **gush** of adjectives, the same incorrigible tendency to estimate his effort according to each writer's personal preferences.*

*And then his success began to **submerge** him: he gasped under the thickening **shower** of letters.*

*And I want to be beforehand now – dam the **flood** before it **swamps** me.*

*Have you any idea of the **deluge** of stuff that people write to a successful novelist?*

*The letters continued to **pour** in for several weeks after the appearance of "Abundance."*

2 Choose the correct keyword to complete the sentences below.

1 The company received a *deluge/pour* of complaints about the defective product.
2 On-line bookshops were *gushed/swamped* with orders during the pre-Christmas rush.
3 I opened the curtains and light *flooded/deluge* into the room.
4 He opened the door of the cupboard and a *swamp/shower* of dust fell out on his head.
5 He felt a sudden *gush/submerge* of love for her.
6 She wanted to *flood/submerge* herself in her writing.

Praise and recognition described in terms of food and eating

Another common metaphor repeated throughout the story is that of praise as food.

3 Look at the extracts below. Match the key words in bold with their definitions.

*He had found a **savour** even in the grosser evidences of popularity.*

*He had **gulped** the praise of "Diadems and Faggots" as undiscriminatingly as it was offered.*

*Now he knew for the first time the subtler pleasures of the **palate**.*

*Such false humility was less excusable than the crudest **appetite** for praise.*

*At first he was conscious only of a vague **hunger**, but in time the **craving** resolved into a shame-faced desire to see his letters.*

1. the natural feeling of wanting to eat
2. a very strong feeling of wanting something specific to eat
3. to swallow food or drink very quickly in a way that shows that you are very hungry
4. a feeling that you have when you need to eat something
5. the ability to taste and judge the flavours in food or drinks
6. (*formal*) a flavour or smell, especially a pleasant one

4 Look at these common expressions using the concepts of food and eating. Underline the key words. What concept are they describing?

1. We have yet to experience the sweet smell of success.
2. The public's appetite for celebrity gossip seems insatiable.
3. The senator talked about America's hunger for leadership.
4. He craved for the attention of the older children.
5. He found the criticism hard to swallow.
6. People are hungry for news.
7. Even at a young age he had a taste for books.
8. After 16 years in prison, it was their first taste of freedom.

Do you use similar metaphors in your language? How would you translate the expressions in 1–8 above?

Formal language

The author often uses formal language to describe the day to day routines and activities of the characters.

5 Match the formal words in bold in the examples below with the informal equivalents in the box.

be back   chose   come   examples   handwriting   show you
time   told   want   work   understood   help

*The two notes looked harmless enough, and the **calligraphy** of one was vaguely familiar.*

*"I could **submit** a few **specimens**," he suggested.*

*"When do you **wish** me to begin?"*

*A telegram **apprised** him one morning that Vyse would **return to his post** that day.*

*"You'll remember that ten was the **hour** you **appointed** for the secretaries to **call**, sir."*

*I **inferred** from your advertisement that you want someone to **relieve** you in your literary work.*

6 Compare the two sentences below. The first is taken from the story. The second is a simpler, less formal version. Notice the changes made to replace the words in bold.

a) *The valet opened the door **to announce** "Mr. Vyse," and Betton, a moment later, **crossed the threshold** of his pleasant library.*

b) The valet opened the door to say that Mr Vyse had arrived and Betton, a moment later, walked into the library.

7 Rewrite the following sentences in a simpler, more direct style, replacing the words and phrases in bold with more informal equivalents.

1 *Betton began to wonder if Vyse were **exercising an unauthorized discrimination** keeping back the **communications** he **deemed least important**.*

2 *The secretary, suddenly **advised of** his father's illness, **asked permission** to **absent himself** for a fortnight.*

3 *It **contained no allusion**, however indirect, to the special **purport** of his **appeal**.*

4 *It was the worst part of his **plight** that his first success had **goaded** him to **the perpetration of this particular folly**.*

5 *For ten days he **tasted the furtive joy** of a first **perusal of his letters**.*

Idiomatic expressions

8 Look at these idiomatic expressions and match them to the definitions 1–8 below.

dread the sight of something
Betton about his fan letters:

*"How I used to **dread the sight** of my letter-box!"*

strike a note/the right note
Vyse about the style of the letters he's going to write for Betton:
*"If I've **struck the note** I won't bother you again," he urged.*

see straight through something
Betton thinking about how to tell Vyse he doesn't need him anymore:
*"If I tell him I've no use for him now, **he'll see straight through it**, of course."*

drive at something
Betton to Vyse when Vyse first talks to him about the hoax letters:
*"**What** the devil **are you driving at**?" he asked.*

at the mercy of something
Betton in response to the hoax letters from the professor:
*It was ridiculous to try to do conscientious work if one's self-esteem were **at the mercy of** popular judgments.*

touch and go
Vyse talking about his father's illness:
*"Yes – it was **touch and go** when I got there."*

put someone on their guard
Betton to Vyse about the hoax letters he sent himself:
*"you'd foolishly **put me on my guard** by pointing out to me that they were a clumsy forgery."*

an eye for an eye
Betton, asking Vyse why he wrote the hoax letters:
"What is it, then? The joy of uncovering my nakedness? An eye for an eye? Is it that?"

stone/stony broke
Vyse at the end of the story, explaining his behaviour:
*"I'm **stone broke**, and wanted to keep my job – that's what it is," he said wearily.*

1 what someone really wants to say
2 not look forward to seeing something
3 the idea that someone who has harmed another person should be punished by having the same thing done to them
4 in a situation that is controlled by someone or something with the power to harm you
5 to make you think to behave more carefully
6 to recognise that something is not true and not be tricked by it
7 to create a particular mood by the way that you speak or behave
8 you don't have any money

9 **Use the expressions on the previous page to complete these sentences.**

1 He managed to .... the right .... in the letter, neither too formal nor too friendly.
2 I'm always .... in January – I spend so much on Christmas presents for all the family!
3 I didn't really understand what he was .... when he said he'd seen it all before.
4 It was a case of .... – he broke my bike so I smashed his car!
5 I hated school when I was in my teens – I always .... of the school-bus in the mornings.
6 Our tent was blown away in the storm and we were left .... of the wind and rain with no protection or shelter.
7 He .... my lies and excuses and didn't believe a word I said.
8 He knew something strange must be happening. The sight of the police van at the corner of the street had ....

Literary analysis

Plot

1 Number the events below in the order in which they happened.
   a) Betton wrote his second novel
   b) Betton's second novel was published
   c) The second novel received a lot of criticism
   d) Betton advertised for a secretary to deal with his fan letters
   e) Vyse took the job as secretary
   f) Vyse wrote his first novel
   g) Betton offered to show Vyse's novel to a publisher
   h) Betton started a career in business
   i) Vyse started a career in business
   j) Betton wrote some false fan letters
   k) Vyse wrote some false fan letters
2 What do you think is/are the most important event/s ? Why?
3 Think about these questions. When did you, as a first-time reader, realise that Betton had written the first hoax letters? When did Vyse understand that Betton had written the letters to himself? When did you, as a first-time reader, realise that Vyse was writing hoax letters to Betton? When did Betton find out? Do you think he suspected anything earlier? What does this tell us about Betton and Vyse?

4 In what ways do Betton and Vyse's lives mirror each other?
5 What is the significance of the title, 'Full Circle'? What has come full circle at the end of the story? What do you think will happen next?

Character

6 There are three characters in the story. Who are they? What do we know about them? What are their relationships to each other? Who is the main character?
7 Look at the adjectives in the box. They are all used in the story to describe the three men. Which character is each adjective used to describe?

| affable calm devoted furious hard up high-coloured pale shabby starved stout thin truculent watchful well-fed |

Look again at the adjectives used to describe Betton and Vyse. Find pairs of opposites. Write them in the columns below.
Betton   Vyse
affable (= friendly and relaxed)   *truculent* (= easily annoyed)
In what other ways are the two men different from each other?
8 Which of the adjectives below would you choose to describe Betton? Think about his reactions to becoming famous, his reactions to the criticism of his second novel and his treatment of Vyse.

| vain confident sensitive generous insecure intelligent self-absorbed modest lazy selfish |

Can you think of any more adjectives that sum up his character? Do you think Betton is a positive character? What are his strengths and his weaknesses? Do you think you would get on well with him if you met him? Why/why not?
9 Why did you think Vyse wrote the hoax letters? What do you think is Vyse's opinion of Betton? Does he like him? Why/why not?
10 Most of the explanations for Vyse's behaviour and the interpretations of his thoughts and motives come from Betton. Do you think that Betton's interpretation is correct? Or is he making things more complicated than they really are?
11 Which man do you sympathise with most, Betton or Vyse? Why?

Narration

12 Who is telling the story? Does the narrator introduce him/herself? Is the narrator objective?
13 Does the narrator report the thoughts and feelings of all the characters? Whose point of view is most important? What effect does this have on the way the story is told?
14 There is a lot of dialogue in the story. Who does most of the talking? What does this tell us about the characters and about the focus of the story?
15 The narrator does not, at any point, give us a direct physical description of Betton. Think about how the narrator uses Betton's actions, thoughts and speech to describe him, both physically and psychologically. What effect does this have?
16 In what way would the story be told differently if Vyse or Strett were the narrators, or the main focus of the narration?

Style

17 Look at the first page of the story when the author is setting the scene and the tone for the story. List the examples of luxury and comfort in Betton's new lifestyle, for example the *warm, red carpet*. Notice the language used to describe the sounds on the street and the luxury of his private bathroom.
Find words that mean:
in a very slow and relaxed manner [paragraph 3]
physical pleasure [paragraph 4]
making you feel refreshed [paragraph 4]
What is the effect of these words on the description?
18 Look at the descriptions below and answer the questions.
   a) What is being described in each case?
   b) What is it being compared to?
   c) What is the effect?
   d) What does it tell us about Betton and his lifestyle?

the sound had been like music to him: the complex orchestration to which the tune of his new life was set
the hours hunted him like a pack of blood-hounds
entering the shining tiled sanctuary where his great porcelain bath proffered[63] its renovating flood
his blue and white temple of refreshment

---

[63] *formal*: to offer someone something

19 In the initial description of Betton's lifestyle and his attitude to it, two things are compared and contrasted:
   – his new life with his former life
   – his attitude to his new life at the beginning and his attitude now.
   a) What do these contrasts tell us about Betton?
   b) What impression do we get of him?
   c) How does the language used by the author contribute to this impression?

20 When the author is describing Betton's reactions to the success of his first novel she uses an unusual and elaborate metaphor (see *Language study* section for more on the use of metaphors).
   When their thick broth of praise was strained through the author's anxious vanity there remained to him so small a sediment of definite specific understanding!
   a) What is the image that is created by the metaphor?
   b) What effect does it have?
   c) What does it tell us about Betton's "anxious vanity"?
   Later the author describes Betton's newfound pleasure in reading the letters written in response to his second novel. Analyse the metaphor using the questions above.
   It was really a pleasure to read them, now that he was relieved of the burden of replying: his new relation to his correspondents had the glow of a love-affair unchilled by the contingency[64] of marriage.

21 Dialogue plays an important part in the story. Look at the first exchange between Betton and Vyse [page 156]. Compare the way the two men speak. Who speaks most? Who is the more businesslike of the two? As the conversation continues Betton becomes embarrassed and uncomfortable. Why? How do you think Vyse feels? What does the conversation tell us about the two men and their relationship to each other?

22 Vyse is a man of few words, but sometimes the author uses his words to comment on the main themes of the story. For example, when Vyse is showing Betton an example of his writing he comments that: *It's wonderful how little people see.*
   Think about how this comment relates to the misunderstandings in the story and the themes of vanity and ego.

Guidance to the above literary terms, answer keys to all the exercises and activities, plus a wealth of other reading-practice material, can be found on the student's section of the Macmillan Readers website at: www.macmillanenglish.com/readers.

64 possibility

Essay questions

Language analysis

> Discuss how one or more of the language areas you have studied help contribute to the telling of two OR MORE of the stories in the collection.

Analysing the question

What is the question asking?

It is asking you to:
- choose one or more language areas from the index
- explain how these language areas function in the context of storytelling
- use examples from two or more of the stories in the collection.

Preparing your answer

1 Look back through the *Language analysis* sections of the stories you have read and choose one or more language areas that you feel confident about.
2 Make notes about the language areas. Include notes on form, function and use.
3 Choose examples from at least two stories. Choose examples from both classic and contemporary stories, if possible.
4 Look back at the question and your notes and plan your essay. Use the structure of the question to structure your essay. Here is an example:

Introduction	Introduce the area you are going to describe.
Main body 1	Explain the general function of the areas you have chosen, use examples from both stories.
Main body 2	Analyse how the areas contribute to the style and atmosphere of both stories, referring to specific passages in the stories.
Conclusion	Summarise the literary use and function of the language areas you focused on.

Literary analysis

Choose and contrast the settings of two of the stories in the collection.

Analysing the question

What is the question asking?

It is asking you to:
- look at two stories in the collection
- describe the setting of the story in each collection
- describe any similarities and differences.

Preparing your answer

1 Choose two stories from this collection. Make notes about the setting of these stories – when and where the story takes place. Look at descriptions of places, people, the language used, the atmosphere, and the main themes.
2 Find key scenes in the story where the setting plays an important part. Make a note of any useful quotations.
3 Make a list of similarities and differences between the stories: think about the time of year, the social environment, (city, country, suburbs etc.), social class, the historical context, and so on.
4 Read the question again and write a plan for your essay. Here is an example:

Introduction	Briefly introduce the two stories.
Story 1	Describe the first story and its setting. How do time and place affect the development of the story?
Story 2	Describe the second story and its setting. How do time and place affect the development of the story?
Similarities	Discuss the similarities between the setting of the two stories.
Differences	Discuss the differences between the setting of the two stories.
Conclusion	Make a general comment about the importance of the setting in a short story.

Glossary

The definitions in the glossary refer to the meanings of the words and phrases as they are used in the short stories in this collection. Some words and phrases may also have other meanings which are not given here. The definitions are arranged in the story in which they appear, and in alphabetical order.

The Gift of the Magi

adorn (v) decorate
cascade (n) *mainly literary* a small waterfall or something that hangs down in large amounts
chaste (adj) *mainly literary* innocent and pure
coax (v) to make something such as a machine or piece of equipment do what you want it to do by being skilful, gentle and patient
contract (v) to become smaller
crave (v) to want something very much in a way that is very hard to control
dim (adj) not bright, with very little light
dully (adv) without showing or feeling interest
enfold (v) *formal* to surround or enclose someone or something
falter (v) to stop doing something because you have lost your confidence or determination
fixedly (adv) to look at something without paying attention to anything else
garment (n) *formal* a piece of clothing
have someone going PHRASE to make someone feel confused or worried
laboriously (adj) doing something slowly because you find it difficult
longitudinal (adj) going from the top to the bottom of something
manger (n) a long low open container that horse or cows eat from (according to the New Testament, the baby Jesus was put to lie in a manger)

nimble (adj) able to move quickly and easily
on the sly PHRASE *informal* done secretly, especially because you think you shouldn't be doing it
pant (v) to breathe very loudly with your mouth open, for example when you have been running
patent (adj) extremely obvious
proclaim (v) to be a clear sign of something
ravages (n) damage or destruction (usually caused by war, disease or weather)
shrunk (shrink) (v) became smaller in size
singed (adj) burned
subside (v) to become weaker, less violent or less severe
tortoise shell (n) the hard shell of a type of turtle that is brown and orange and is used for making things like jewellery
turn something inside out PHRASE to search a place very thoroughly
truant (adj) staying away from school without permission
unassuming (adj) showing approval – behaving in a quiet and pleasant way, without trying to appear better or more important than other people
wriggle (v) to move by twisting or turning quickly
yearn (v) *mainly literary* to want something a lot, especially something that you know you may not be able to have

The Lost Phœbe

ample (adj) enough, and often more than you need

apparition (n) *formal* a strange image or creature that someone sees

arouse (v) to cause an emotion or attitude

baggy (adj) baggy clothes are very loose on your body

bloom (v) if a tree or plant blooms, it produces flowers that have opened

briskly (adv) moving or acting quickly

brooding (adj) to brood is to think and worry about something a lot

bustle (v) to do something or go somewhere quickly, usually because you are very busy

chill (adj) very cold

chink (n) a very small space in a wall

clothes press (n) a piece of furniture with drawers and a cupboard where you can keep clothes

clothes-horse (n) a frame of wooden or plastic bars on which you hang wet clothes so that they can dry inside your house

commonplace (adj) not unusual

creaky (adj) if something creaks, especially something wooden, it makes a high noise when it moves or when you put weight on it

creed (n) *formal* a set of religious beliefs

crook cane (n) a long stick that is curved at one end

crumbling (adj) to crumble is to fall gradually into pieces

cumbersome (adj) large, heavy, difficult to move or carry

deem (v) *formal* considered

demented (adj) *informal* behaving in a strange, stupid or crazy way

dolefully (adv) sadly

duly (adv) *formal* in the way that you expect or think is appropriate

elated (adj) extremely happy and excited

endurable (adj) able to be suffered in a patient way over a long period

evade (v) to avoid accepting or dealing with something that you should do

fallow (adj) land that has been ploughed but does not have crops growing on it

fate (n) the things that happen to someone, especially unpleasant things

feeble (adj) not strong enough to be seen or heard clearly

ferret (n) a small, thin furry animal with a long tail that is sometimes used for hunting rabbits

flick (v) to make something move quickly and suddenly, especially with a quick movement of the hand

flicker (v) to go on and off

four poster bed (n) an old-fashioned bed with four tall posts at the corners

fulfilment (n) the act of doing something that is promised or expected

ghost (n) the spirit of a dead person that someone sees or hears

glint (n) a sudden quick appearance of a strong emotion such as anger in someone's eyes

gloomy (adj) feeling sad and without hope

grumble (v) to complain

halo (n) a circle of light around the head of a holy person in religious paintings

harmless (adj) not likely to upset people or cause problems

haul (v) to pull or carry something heavy from one place to another

homely (adj) *unusual* pleasant in a way that reminds you of home

humble (adj) not proud, and not thinking that you are better than other people

idly (adv) to be idle is to do nothing

jest (v) *old-fashioned* to speak in a way that is not serious

leap (v) to jump into the air or over a long distance

Macmillan Literature Collections: Glossary

lichen (n) a small, soft plant that grows on surfaces such as trees and walls

log (n) a thick piece of wood cut from a tree

loom (n) a machine used for weaving cloth

mislay (v) to lose something for a time, especially because you can't remember where you put it

moss (n) a soft green or brown plant that grows in a layer on wet ground, rocks or trees

omen (n) a sign that you believe shows whether something good or bad will happen in the future

orchard (n) an area of land where fruit trees are grown

outhouse (n) a separate building that belongs to a house and is used, for example, for keeping animals or equipment in

peer (v) to look very carefully, especially because something is difficult to see

perspiring (adj) producing liquid on your skin as a result of being hot, sick or nervous

pierced (adj) to pierce something is to make a hole in it

pleading (n) *unusual* asking for something in an urgent or emotional way

precipice (n) a very steep high cliff

protuberant (adj) *formal* much further forward than the rest of something

query (n) a question that you ask because you want information or because you are not certain about something

quiver (v) to shake with short, quick movements

ragged (adj) torn and dirty

reminiscent (adj) reminding you of people or experiences in your past

reproach (v) to criticize and feel disappointed with someone for something they have done

retort (v) to reply immediately in an angry or humorous way to something someone has said

roam (v) to move or travel with no particular purpose

rocking chair (n) a chair that has two carved pieces under it so that when someone sits on it they can move it backward and forward

rouse (v) to wake up

scramble (v) to climb somewhere using your feet and hands

shaggy (adj) long, thick and messy

slab (n) a large, flat piece of a hard material such as stone or wood

solace (n) something that makes you feel better when you are sad or upset

sorrow (n) great sadness

spectral (adj) *mainly literary* looking like a ghost, for example by being very thin and pale

speculative (adj) based on guesses or on a little information, not on facts

squeak (v) to make a short, high noise

staggering (adj) extremely surprising

stamp (v) to walk putting your feet down hard and noisily on the ground, usually because you are angry

stout (adj) slightly fat

strain (v) to try very hard to do something

sturdy (adj) strong and not easily hurt, damaged or affected by what happens

thrill (v) *formal* to feel very excited and pleased

tin (adj) made of a soft, light, silver metal

tingle (v) if part of your body tingles, it stings slightly because you are hot, cold, afraid etc

tramp (v) to walk slowly for a long distance

unkempt (adj) dirty and messy

wean (v) to make someone gradually stop depending on something

weary (adj) very tired

weather (v) to manage a difficult experience without being seriously harmed

weird (adj) strange and unusual, sometimes in a way that upsets you

whip (n) a long, thin piece of leather with a handle on one end used for making horses move faster or for hitting someone

will (n) a legal document that explains what you want to happen to your money and possessions after you die

wind (v) the action of turning a part of a clock or watch to make it operate

wisp (n) something that has a long, thin delicate shape, for example a cloud, smoke or hair

wretched (adj) very bad

The Baby Party

abrupt (adj) sudden and unexpected, often in an unpleasant way

blow (n) a hard hit from someone's hand or an object

bruise (n) a mark you get on your body if you are hit or if you knock against something

cherish (v) to think that something is important and to wish to keep it

contempt (n) failure to show respect

curse (v) to use offensive or impolite language

defiance (n) a refusal to obey a person or a rule

defunct (adj) not existing or working any more

disrupt (v) to interrupt something and prevent it from continuing by creating a problem

flushed (adj) a pink colour

frown (v) to have your eyebrows down and closer together because you are annoyed, worried, or thinking hard

giggle (v) to laugh in a nervous, excited or silly way that is difficult to control

huddle (v) to move close together in order to stay warm, feel safe or talk

indignation (n) anger at an unfair situation or about someone's unfair behaviour

inscrutable (adj) when someone is inscrutable, it is impossible to understand what they are thinking from their expression or what they say

jovial (adj) cheerful and friendly

manoeuvre (n) an action or movement that you need skill or care to do

meek (adj) quiet, gentle, easily persuaded by other people to do what they want

patter (n) a series of short quiet sounds caused by something falling onto or hitting a surface or by someone walking or running

pretence (n) a way of behaving that does not express your real feelings

prospect (n) the possibility that something will happen, especially something good

rough (adj) not gentle, violent

shrewd (adj) able to judge situations very well and make good decisions

snort (n) a sudden loud noise that you make through your nose, for example because you are angry or laughing

sob (n) the sound someone makes when they cry noisily while taking short breaths

sulkily (adv) in a way that shows you are unhappy or angry and not wanting to talk to anyone or be with other people

swollen (adj) bigger in size as a result of injury or illness

tiptoe (v) to stand or walk on your toes

tremble (v) to shake, especially because you are nervous, afraid or excited

urge (v) to advise someone very strongly about what action or attitude they should take
weary (adj) very tired or tiring

You Were Perfectly Fine

chintz (n) cotton cloth with a pattern of flowers used especially for curtains and chair covers
clam (n) a small shellfish
cradle (n) a small bed for a baby
damp (adj) something that is damp is slightly wet, often in an unpleasant way or when it should be dry
humming-bird (n) a very small brightly coloured bird that makes a low, continuous noise when it moves its wings
mastiff (n) a large, strong dog with short, smooth fur
nasty (adj) unkind or offensive
overwhelming (adj) much larger, stronger, more important etc. than anything else in a situation
sidewalk (n) *American* an area along the side of a street that has a hard surface, used by people who are walking
soul (n) the spiritual part of a person that most religions believe continues to exist after their body dies

The Romantic

awareness (n) the ability to notice things
awkward (adj) difficult to deal with and embarrassing
browse (v) to look at things without looking for anything in particular
brunch (n) a meal that combines breakfast and lunch and is usually served in the late morning
bump (v) to accidentally hit part of your body against something making it hurt

chuck (v) *informal* to throw out; get rid of something that you don"t want
creased (adj) marked with lines
fatigue (n) feeling of being extremely tired
fuss (over something) (v) to give something a lot of attention
hang-up (n) something that you are worried or embarrassed about, especially something that is not very important
harm (n) injury, damage or problems caused by something you do
hazy (adj) not clear, vague
hurdle (n) one of several problems that you must solve before you can do something successfully
in a daze PHRASE unable to think clearly or understand what is happening because you are surprised, tired, upset or have been hit on the head
jolly (adj) friendly and cheerful
lightweight (adj) not serious or important
linger (v) to stay somewhere longer or spend longer doing something than necessary for your own enjoyment or benefit
mishap (n) a minor mistake or accident
mugging (n) an attack on someone in a public place in order to steal their money, jewellery or other
odds and ends PHRASE small things that are all different and not valuable or important
pang (n) a very strong, sudden and unpleasant pain or emotion
perk up (v) to begin to feel happier or more lively
perky (adj) *informal* lively and happy
pop over (v) to go somewhere for a short time
put oneself out (for someone) PHRASE to do something to help someone even if it causes problems and difficulties for you

rags (n) pieces of old cloth used for cleaning or wiping something

run up (v) to make something quickly, especially something you sew

shy away from (v) to avoid someone

shudder (v) if you shudder, your body suddenly shakes, for example because you feel cold or frightened

spot (v) to notice

stocky (adj) describes a person who looks strong but not tall

stuck (adj) caught or held in a position so that you can't move

tackle (v) to make an organised and determined attempt to deal with a problem

tied up (adj) very busy

Full Circle

accomplished (adj) good at doing something that needs a lot of skill

affable (adj) friendly, relaxed and easy to get on with

assent (n) to agree with or officially give permission

baffled (adj) confused

blotchy (adj) covered in dark marks or stains

bravado (n) a brave and confident way of behaving, especially when you do not really feel like this

champion (v) to publicly support a person

charity bazaar (n) a sale, especially of used goods, to raise money for a particular project or organisation

congested (adj) blocked with blood or another liquid

conjecture (n) a theory or guess based on incomplete information

crackling (adj) used to describe repeated short, hard sounds

craving (n) a very strong feeling of wanting something

dam (v) to stop a river or stream from flowing by a wall across it

deem (v) consider to be

deluge (n) a very heavy fall of rain

denunciation (n) very strong public criticism of someone or something

descent (n) the act of moving down to a lower place or position

diametrically (adv) completely different from each other

embittered (adj) angry and unhappy about things that have happened to you in the past

fake (v) to make a copy of something in order to trick people

feign (v) pretend you don't feel a particular emotion

female suffrage (n) women's right to vote

forger (n) a person who commits the crime of **forgery**

forgery (n) a document, painting, work of art etc that is a copy of the original, and has illegally been presented as the original. **clumsy forgery** – not a very good copy

fret (v) to worry about something continuously

fume (v) to feel or show a lot of anger

furtive (adj) done quickly and secretly to avoid being noticed

gasp (v) to breathe in suddenly, for example because you are surprised, shocked or in pain

goad (v) to encourage someone to act

grind (v) to work hard and in a determined way

groan (n) a long low sound that a person makes, especially when they are in pain or unhappy

groaningly (adv) see **groan**

grope (v) search for an idea or something to say

growl (v) to say something in an unfriendly and angry way

grudge (n) a feeling of anger towards somebody because they have done something to you that does not seem right or fair

hard up (adj) not having a lot of money

Macmillan Literature Collections: Glossary

hearth (n) fireplace
heartiness (n) sincerity
high-coloured (adj) with a red face
humbug (n) behaviour or talk that is not sincere
imperturbable (adj) always calm and not easily upset
inane (adj) completely stupid
incorrigible (adj) someone who is incorrigible does bad things or has bad habits and won't change
insidiously (adv) seemingly innocent, but actually dangerous
inscrutable (adj) if someone is inscrutable it is impossible to understand what they are thinking or feeling from their expression or what they say
interject (v) to say something suddenly that interrupts someone else who is speaking
jeer (v) to shout or laugh at someone in an unkind way
jerk open (v) to pull something open suddenly using a lot of force
latent (adj) something that is latent exists but is not obvious and has not developed yet
lingeringly (adv) slowly
lull (n) a short period of calm or lessened activity
mauve (adv) pale purple in colour
mindful of (adj) careful about, or conscious of
nape (n) the back of your neck
nudge (v) to use a part of your body, especially your elbow, to give a little push to someone
oblivion (n) a state in which someone or something has been completely forgotten
plaintively (adv) sadly
plight (n) a sad, serious or difficult situation
plunge (n) a jump or dive into water
preponderate (v) to be more important than other things
preposterous (adj) extremely unreasonable or silly
promiscuous (adj) shared by a lot of people
puerile (adj) childish
riveted (adj) so interested in something that it takes all your attention
ruddy (adj) red in colour
sardonically (adv) with irony or sarcasm
savour (n) *formal:* a flavour or smell, especially a pleasant one
scathingly (adv) extremely critically
shabby (adj) old and in bad condition, unfair or dishonest
shabbiness (n) see shabby
shallow (adj) with only a short distance from the top or surface to the bottom
shamefaced (adj) with an expression that shows you feel ashamed or embarrassed about something
sheepishly (adv) feeling ashamed or embarrassed about something
shrinkage (n) the process of becoming smaller in size
shudder (n) a quick, uncontrolled shaking movement
sneer (n) an unpleasant smile that shows you do not respect someone or something
solace (n) something that makes you feel better when you are sad or upset
specimen (n) an example of something
stammer (v) to keep repeating a sound or have difficulty saying certain words because of a speech problem, nervousness, excitement etc
stock-still (adj) not making any movements
stout (adj) slightly fat
swamp (v) to fill or cover something in water
sway (v) influence

temper (v) *formal:* to make something less strong or extreme

toss something down (v) to throw something down in a careless way

twinge (n) a sudden, short feeling of emotion or pain, especially an unpleasant one

unappeasable (adj) always wanting more and never feeling satisfied

unguarded (adj) saying or doing something without thinking first

unsparing (adj) does not hide unpleasant details

unworthy (adj) not to deserve something

uproarious (adj) extremely noisy and loud

vindictive (adj) someone who is vindictive is cruel to anyone who hurts them and will not forgive them

vow (v) to promise that you will do something

Dictionary extracts adapted from the Macmillan English Dictionary © Macmillan Publishers 2002

Language study index

The Gift of the Magi
Past perfect simple, simple and past perfect continuous	26
Past perfect inversion in continuous sentences	27
Fronting as a literary device	28
Inversion after fronting	28

The Lost Phœbe
The use of simile and metaphor	63
Compound adjectives	63
Multiple-clause sentences	65
The use of preposition + *which*	66

The Baby Party
Adverbs of manner	92
Present participles in adverbial clauses	93

You Were Perfectly Fine
Ellipsis	107
Fronting in informal speech	108
The use of *get*	108

The Romantic
Discourse markers	136
Formal and informal vocabulary	137
The use of *rather*	138
Clichés	138

Full Circle
Common metaphors	179
Formal language	181
Idiomatic expressions	182

For more information and free resources visit:
www.macmillanenglish.com/readers

MACMILLAN READERS